PRAISE FOR *PEANUT BUTTER PASSION*

Annie's recipes for Peanut Butter Blondies, Peanut Butter Bars, and Peanut Butter Munchies were new to me, but I wanted to do something different for an upcoming social gathering I was having. I whipped these three delights up and *all* were hits! They were so simple and quick to put together but tasted as though they came from a gourmet bake shop. The Peanut Butter Munchies were my personal favorite; they are like little bites of heaven, and I promise you can't eat just one!
~ Erin Kirkland, Owner, Southern Yankee Cupcake

Peanut Butter Passion is filled with decadent and delicious recipes that you will want to make over and over again. Ann does a fantastic job of presenting creative and diverse recipes that utilize perfect techniques, and are easy to follow. She has managed to bring everyone's favorite peanut butter into a plethora of different meal courses and different forms of dessert. I cannot wait to try more of Ann's recipes at home and in our bakery!
-Ken Schenk, baker & owner, The Pennsylvania Bakery in Camp Hill, PA

PEANUT
BUTTER
Passion

A Peanut Butter Lover's Cookbook

ANN CRISS

Mill City Press, Inc.
322 First Avenue N, 5th floor
Minneapolis, MN 55401
612.455.2293
www.millcitypublishing.com

ISBN-13: 978-1-63413-717-1
LCCN: 2015912227

Cover Design by Sophie Chi
Typeset by Lois Stanfield

Printed in the United States of America

This book is dedicated to my husband, Jim, who has supported me throughout the entire process, including many years of talking about the cookbook, gathering recipes, the documentation process, and finally evaluating and finding the right publisher. I am grateful for his love, encouragement and support each and every day.

ACKNOWLEDGMENTS

. . . . .

I would like to acknowledge my 90-year-old father, Jim Crawford, who arranged for me to meet with a retired publisher, Marge Keen, in the retirement community where he resides. Marge's input was invaluable and so was the book she gave me to read, *The Fine Print of Self-Publishing* by Mark Levine. This book is written for anyone interested in self-publishing and evaluates the basics of self-publishing, as well as reviews many publishing companies and the services they offer. Reading and re-reading this book narrowed the field when it came to choosing a publisher. The thorough and expert knowledge provided in this book and a personal phone call with the author, Mark Levine, helped with my decision to choose Mill City Press as the publisher of *Peanut Butter Passion*.

I also wish to extend a special thank you to all my friends and family who encouraged me and provided me with recipes! **YOU KNOW WHO YOU ARE!**

INTRODUCTION

· · · ·

Let's go back about 22 years, as if it was yesterday, and my supervisor, Beth Kammer, called and said, "I want you to take off tomorrow." I had reached my limit in vacation hours and I was about to begin losing my accumulated time. "I hope you can find something fun to do on such short notice," she said. "Oh, I will. I'll work on my cookbook." "That doesn't sound like fun. Tell me you are going to walk the dog or something," Beth replied. "I'll do that too," I said.

The next day I spent two hours working on the cookbook, and it brought back fun filled memories of family gatherings, food gifts from special people, and food gifts for special people. It also brought excitement and anticipation of the joy I would receive if I could share all of these recipes with other people, specifically, other peanut butter lovers!

I have been collecting recipes for many years, and not just peanut butter recipes. My initial collection is still in the shoe box where I first began to save recipes. I progressed to index cards in beautifully designed recipe boxes, and then on to three ring binders with plastic cover sheets and dividers, separating appetizers from main courses and salads from desserts. I now have two cupboards full of cookbooks, recipes and binders. And I keep collecting!

My friends continue to bring me peanut butter recipes because I have talked about my "Peanut Butter Cookbook" for so long. I imagine some have lost all hope that I would ever begin it, let alone ever complete it. But I have recently begun a new chapter in my life, retirement, and I could not think of a better way to continue life's journey than by doing something I love to do!

IT'S NOW OR NEVER!

As a peanut butter lover, I have been experimenting with different recipes for years. Some have become favorites, not just of mine, but of friends and family alike. When you see the word *favorite* in bold italics at the bottom of a recipe, you will know it is one of my favorites and more than likely many others, too! Certain family gatherings require a special dessert from me and I better not show up empty-handed. As my cousin would say, "Annie always brings the Chips of Chocolate Peanut Butter Cake or John's Secret Peanut Butter Cake," made fresh, so that it is still warm when I arrive. The smell creates the anticipation for desire and, once tasted, the memory returns. It is as good, if not better, than remembered!

When I first began thinking about compiling my recipes in to a cookbook, I mentioned it to family. I then tested the waters with co-workers and friends. Reactions were mixed! Non-peanut butter lovers could have put a damper on my fire of enthusiasm with their reactions. Looks alone suggested, "Are you crazy? No one would be interested in that." Two fans in particular, Anne Ross and Susanne Ryan, encouraged me to move forward.

I finally realized, what others think of the idea doesn't really matter. This book is a labor of love, dedicated to Peanut Butter Lovers who are drawn to recipes with peanut butter in the ingredients. I hope my passion for Peanut Butter translates into hours of pleasure for many people. As you read the recipes, experiment and savor the taste of the one ingredient that can turn any recipe in to a masterpiece to remember, **PEANUT BUTTER!**

You will find recipes indicating a specific brand of peanut butter and others without. If you have a favorite brand, use it. I use our local Giant brand peanut butter in most of my recipes, unless otherwise specified. All recipes are to be made with creamy peanut butter unless otherwise specified.

I like delicious, but easy. You will find most of these recipes easy and quick, with a few more time-consuming ones interspersed here and there.

This is not a calorie conscious cookbook, but I urge everyone to eat in moderation so you can savor a taste of all these wonderful recipes. I often bake, taste and give away!

I hope the joy I have received in compiling my recipes will become a blessing for many. One thing I plan to do is offer 10 percent of the proceeds to charities. I also plan to approach local Nursing Homes and Retirement Communities that have fundraisers each year and provide them with the opportunity to sell the cookbook at their bazaars and bake sales. I will take back the cookbooks they do not sell and **I WILL GIVE THEM A PORTION ON WHAT THEY SOLD!**

CONTENTS

· · · ·

You might expect most of the recipes in this cookbook to be cookies, candies and desserts. Most of them are, but as my love of peanut butter continued to grow, I began experimenting with a number of recipes from salads and appetizers to main dishes. Don't limit yourself, much as a child who will not eat spinach! Experiment, as I have, and discover new and exciting uses for peanut butter!
I DARE YOU!

BREADS, CEREAL, PANCAKES

OATMEAL BUTTERMILK
PEANUT BUTTER PANCAKES

· · · · ·

1⅓ Cups low-fat or nonfat
 buttermilk
1 Tablespoon vegetable oil
1¼ Cups all-purpose flour
½ teaspoon baking soda
¼ Cup peanut butter chips

½ Cup quick cooking oats
½ teaspoon vanilla
1 large egg, lightly beaten
2 Tablespoons brown sugar
½ teaspoon salt

Combine buttermilk, oats and vanilla; let stand 10 minutes, stirring occasionally. Stir in oil and egg. Lightly spoon flour into dry measuring cups; level with a knife. Combine flour, brown sugar, baking soda, and salt in a large bowl. Add oat mixture to flour mixture, stirring until smooth. Stir in peanut butter chips.

Makes 8 pancakes.

· · · · ·

Variation: Add 1 Cup blueberries instead of peanut butter chips. My own creation too! Just wanted to try a variation and my husband loves it! I hope you do too!

I modified this recipe from a basic pancake recipe, adding the peanut butter chips.

PEANUT BUTTER CHIP PANCAKES

. . . . .

¾ Cup pancake mix
1 egg, lightly beaten
½ Cup peanut butter chips
Pancake syrup and fresh blueberries

1 Tablespoon sugar
½ Cup milk
⅓ Cup chopped pecans

In a bowl, combine pancake mix and sugar. Combine egg and milk; add to the dry ingredients just until moistened. Stir in the chips and nuts. Pour batter by ¼ cupful onto a greased hot griddle. Turn each pancake when bubbles form on top; cook until second side is golden brown. Serve with syrup and blueberries.

2 Servings.

. . . . .

This is a basic pancake recipe to which I added peanut butter chips. A friend suggested I add pecans and blueberries for a "nutty" fruit sensation.

APPLE-PEANUT BUTTER FRENCH TOAST

. . . . .

1 apple, peeled and divided:
  ½ diced and ½ thinly sliced
1 Cup 1% milk
1 Tablespoon apple cider
¼ teaspoon vanilla
¼ teaspoon ground ginger
8 Tablespoons peanut butter,
  divided

⅔ Cup maple syrup
+Kosher salt
3 large eggs, beaten
½ teaspoon cinnamon, plus
  more for sprinkling
8 slices whole wheat bread
+ honey for drizzling
1 Tablespoon butter
  (optional)

Make apple syrup: Combine diced apple, maple syrup, and a pinch of salt in a saucepan over medium-high heat. Bring to a simmer; lower heat so syrup bubbles gently and cook 10 minutes. Remove from heat. Make it ahead: Refrigerate syrup and serve it warm or chilled the next day.

Meanwhile, beat milk with eggs, apple cider, cinnamon, vanilla, ground ginger, and a big pinch of salt in a measuring cup. Pour into a shallow bowl or pie plate.

Spread 4 slices bread with 2 Tablespoons peanut butter each. Top each with thinly sliced apple; drizzle apple with honey (if desired) and sprinkle with cinnamon. Sandwich with remaining 4 slices bread and press together.

Melt butter in a large skillet over medium heat. Working 2 sandwiches at a time, soak sandwiches in milk mixture on each side, letting excess drip off. Cook in skillet about 6 minutes for each side, until browned and warmed through. Cut into halves, if desired. Serve with apple syrup.

Serves 4-6

· · · · ·

Variation: You can also use 2% or whole milk in this recipe, unless you want an extra rich flavor, in which case use cream or half-and-half.

If you love apple with peanut butter on it, you will love this recipe taken from a local newspaper!

PEANUT BUTTER
BREAD

. . . . .

2 Cups un-sifted flour (stir to aerate) 3 tsp. baking powder
½ teaspoon salt ¼ Cup butter, softened
¾ Cup chunky peanut butter ¾ Cup sugar
1 large egg 1 teaspoon vanilla
1 Cup milk

In small bowl, stir together the flour, baking powder and salt. Set aside. In medium bowl, beat together the butter and peanut butter until blended; beat in sugar, then eggs and vanilla. Add the flour mixture with a pastry blender. Mix until fine crumbs form. Add milk and stir just until moistened. Bake in a greased loaf pan 5 x 9 x 3-inch at 350 degrees for 55 to 60 minutes.

. . . . .

*Grandma Gilson gave me this recipe on a torn piece of paper. I made it the first time when I wanted to use up some milk before it soured. It became a **FAVORITE** and is delicious warm!*

OATMEAL WITH
PEANUT BUTTER CHIPS

· · · · ·

Oatmeal, quick cooking
Peanut butter chips

Mixed nuts or any kind of nuts
(preferably lightly salted)

Make oatmeal in microwave (for best results, I use Quaker Quick Oats) as directed on package. (I use ¼ Cup oatmeal to ½ Cup of water. Perfect size for small eaters!)

Can't get the kids to eat oatmeal? Try this! Add a handful of mixed nuts and peanut butter chips, 10 to 20. They melt and add the greatest taste to the oatmeal. Would kids like this with chocolate chips? Of course, they would!

· · · · ·

I came up with this simple recipe to help me eat oatmeal. It made all the difference in the world!

DRINKS

PEANUT BUTTER SMOOTHIE

. . . . .

2 Cups Chocolate Soy or Dark
Chocolate Almond Milk
2 heaping Tablespoons
    peanut butter

2 Cups ice
1 frozen peeled banana
⅓ Cup quick cooking oats
2 Tablespoons ground
    flax meal (optional)

Place all ingredients in a blender and mix thoroughly. Enjoy!

. . . . .

Variation: Use regular chocolate milk or white milk and add cocoa. Add additional peanut butter, chocolate or cocoa to taste.

My husband and I worked on this recipe together. He loves soy and almond milk and I love peanut butter. Together it made a winning combination!

APPETIZERS & SNACKS

EASY, QUICK SNACKS

· · · · ·

Apples with Peanut Butter

Bananas with Peanut Butter

Celery with Peanut Butter, add raisins for an extra treat

Frozen Waffle topped with Peanut Butter and Vanilla Ice Cream

Pear Salad with Peanut Butter—Place lettuce on salad plate. Place a canned pear or two on the plate and add a dollop of peanut butter (My mother often served this when I was growing up).

Potato Chip and Peanut Butter Sandwich—my husband's concoction

Pretzels dipped in Peanut Butter

Graham Crackers with Peanut Butter (vanilla or peanut butter ice cream can be added to this to make an ice cream sandwich)

Crackers with Peanut Butter (Wheat Thins, Ritz, or your favorite)

Dip a teaspoon in the peanut butter jar and then into a box of granola cereal for a quick pick me up or bedtime snack. Of course, it is perfect by itself, right out of the jar (Not a good idea if other people live in your home and are using the same jar of peanut butter)!

Peanut Butter and dried fruit (cranberries, raisins, cherries, blueberries or your favorite dried fruit). A single fruit or in combination with your choice of two or three. Drop a teaspoon of peanut butter into ¼ to ½ cup of fruit.

Peanut Butter and chopped nuts (or add to the dried fruit above)

Last, but not least, my 90 year old father, Jim Crawford, has this at breakfast or as a snack—Toast with peanut butter, butter, sugar and cinnamon or toast with peanut butter, butter and 2 Tablespoons of tapioca pudding, topped with cinnamon. This can be made with crackers, too!

CHEERIO TREATS

. . . . .

3 Tablespoons Parkay Spread
Sticks or Parkay Soft
Margarine
1 package (10½ ounce) Kraft
Miniature Marshmallows
½ Cup peanut butter

5 Cups Cheerios, Toasted or
Whole Grain Oat Cereal
1 Cup candy-coated milk
chocolate candies or
raisins (optional)

Grease 13 × 9-inch pan.

Microwave: Parkay in a large bowl on HIGH 45 seconds or
until melted. Stir in marshmallows. Microwave 1 to 2 minutes
or until smooth, stirring halfway through. Stir in peanut butter.
Stir in cereal and candies immediately; mix lightly until well
coated. Press mixture into prepared pan. Cool. Cut and serve.

Top of Stove (other option): Melt Parkay in 3 quart saucepan on
low heat. Add marshmallows; stir until marshmallows are melted
and mixture is smooth. Remove from heat. Stir in peanut butter.
Continue as directed in MICROWAVE instructions.

Tip: For ease in preparation, spray pan and spatula with no-stick
cooking spray.

. . . . .

This recipe was given to me by my friend, Susanne Ryan, a
constant encourager of this project and a fellow peanut butter
lover!

CHOCOLATE COVERED PEANUT BUTTER AND RITZ CRACKERS

· · · · ·

Ritz Crackers   Peanut butter
Chocolate Candy Melts
   (such as Wilton)

Spread peanut butter between two Ritz crackers. Melt coating
chocolate as directed on package, in double boiler or microwave.
Dip one or two at a time in the melted chocolate. Use a fork
to lift out and place on waxed paper lined cookie sheets. When
hardened, store in a covered plastic container and enjoy! Make as
many as you want!

· · · · ·

Variation: The same can be done with graham crackers!

*The above recipe came from Mary Greiner, a friend from Church.
Bet you can't eat just one!*

CHOCOLATE PEANUT BUTTER ENERGY BARS

. . . . .

½ Cup whole wheat flour
½ teaspoon ground cinnamon
½ Cup creamy or chunky peanut
   butter
2 Tablespoons canola oil
1½ Cups barley flakes or
   rolled oats
½ Cup dry roasted peanuts

½ teaspoon baking soda
1 Cup packed light brown
   sugar
2 large eggs
1 teaspoon pure vanilla extract
¾ Cup dried cranberries
1 Cup semi-sweet chocolate
   chips, divided

Preheat oven to 350 degrees. Spray a 13 X 9-inch pan with cooking spray. In a small bowl, whisk together flour, baking soda, and cinnamon. In a large bowl, mix brown sugar and peanut butter until well combined. Beat in eggs, oil and vanilla. Stir in flour mixture. Add barley flakes (or rolled oats), cranberries, peanuts, and ¾ Cup chocolate chips, stirring to combine. Spread evenly in prepared pan. Bake 20 to 25 minutes, until lightly browned and firm to the touch. Cool completely in pan on wire rack.

In a small bowl, set in a pan of simmering water, melt remaining ¼ Cup chocolate chips, stirring until smooth. With fork, drizzle chocolate over bars; refrigerate until set.

Makes 24 bars.

. . . . .

Peanut butter is known to be an energy booster! This version of the popular "protein bar" makes a great snack. Source unknown.

GRANOLA BARS

· · · ·

½ Cup brown sugar
Pinch of salt
2 Cups quick oats
1 Cup butterscotch chips

1 Cup corn syrup
2 Cups peanut butter
2 Cups crispy rice cereal

In saucepan combine brown sugar, corn syrup and salt and bring to a boil. Remove from heat and add peanut butter, oats, cereal and butterscotch chips. Press into a lightly greased 9 × 13-inch pan and cut into bars.

Makes 24.

· · · · ·

Variations: Chocolate, cinnamon, or peanut butter chips can be substituted, or combined, to taste preference. My vote, peanut butter!

This recipe was modified from a wedding present cookbook.

HOLIDAY
PARTY MIX

· · · · ·

12 ounce box Rice Chex

12 ounce box Cheerios

12 ounce box Kix or Corn Chex

16 ounce box Wheat Chex

16 ounce bag pretzels

2 pounds canned peanuts

1 pound butter

½ Cup vegetable oil

⅓ Cup peanut butter

2 Tablespoons onion salt

4 Tablespoons Worcestershire Sauce

¼ teaspoon Tabasco Sauce

1 Tablespoon garlic salt

2 Tablespoons celery salt

Mix together all cereals, pretzels, and peanuts in large baking pan or roaster. In saucepan, melt together butter, oil, and peanut butter. Add onion salt, Worcestershire Sauce, Tabasco Sauce, garlic salt, celery salt and mix well. Pour over dry ingredients. Bake covered at 200 degrees for 1 hour. Stir and bake uncovered for 1 more hour.

· · · · ·

This recipe was modified from a wedding present cookbook.

PEANUT BUTTER
AND APPLE CRESCENTS

. . . . .

1 (8 count) package crescent rolls
2 Tablespoons sugar
½ Cup powdered sugar
1 apple

Peanut butter
1 teaspoon cinnamon
1–3 teaspoons water

Heat oven to 375 degrees. Combine sugar and cinnamon; set aside. Peel, core and finely chop the apple. Separate dough into 8 triangles; spread a thin layer of peanut butter on each triangle. Sprinkle 1 Tablespoon of the chopped apple and 1 teaspoon of the sugar mixture on each triangle. Roll loosely from shortest side of each triangle to the opposite point. Place rolls on ungreased cookie sheet; curve to crescent shape. Bake 10 to 15 minutes until golden brown. Cool 1 minute. Remove from cookie sheet. Stir powdered sugar and 1 to 3 teaspoons water until smooth; drizzle over warm rolls.

. . . . .

Peanut butter and apples again! A great combination! I found this in my collection of recipes, but I have no documentation as to where it originated.

PEANUT BUTTER-CHOCOLATE CRESCENT ROLLS

. . . . .

2 (8 pack) packages of crescent rolls   Peanut butter
Semi-sweet chocolate chips to taste

Separate dough into 16 triangles and spread with peanut butter. Top peanut butter with chocolate chips. Roll and bake at 375 degrees for 10 to 15 minutes until golden brown.

. . . . .

Variations: Roll in powdered sugar after baked. Use peanut butter chips with the chocolate chips or use peanut butter and your favorite jelly.

You can't go wrong with peanut butter and chocolate! Consider serving these warm with vanilla ice cream! This recipe was also found in my "collection of peanut butter recipes" but I do not know the source.

PEANUT BUTTER
CHEX MIX

. . . . .

2 Cups Chex Mix
2 Tablespoons margarine
½ to 1 Cup raisins

2 Tablespoons peanut butter
Peanuts, 4 ounces

Gradually toss in 2 Cups Chex Mix with peanuts. Bake at 250 degrees for 15 minutes. Mix in peanut butter and softened margarine and bake an additional 20 minutes. Cool. Toss in raisins.

. . . . .

Jane Kestner, the dietician from my hospital days, gave me this delicious snack recipe. She used to bring it in to our "Team Conference" meetings and made the long day bearable!

PEANUT BUTTER
RICE KRISPIES

· · · · ·

4 Cups Rice Krispies
½ Cup sugar

1 Cup Light Karo Syrup
½ Cup peanut butter

Spray 8" or 9" square baking pan with cooking spray. Pour cereal into large bowl. Combine sugar and Karo Syrup in medium saucepan. Bring to a boil over medium heat, stirring occasionally. Remove from heat. Stir in peanut butter until smooth. Pour over cereal. Stir to coat well. Press into pan. Cool 15 minutes. Invert onto cutting board. Cut into squares. Store in airtight container.

· · · · ·

Sue Romberger from Sunday School Class offered this recipe! She said, "I think you will like this." Of course, I do! It has peanut butter in it!

PEANUT BUTTER
PROTEIN SNACK

· · · · ·

1½ Cups peanut butter
1¼ Cups rolled oats (toasted)
2 TBSP Nutella
1 Cup mixed nuts, crushed
   (or favorite nuts)

1 Cup honey
1 packet favorite oatmeal
   (Maple Brown Sugar)
½ Cup granola or trail mix

In baking pan, toast oats and nuts at 425 degrees for 15 minutes. Depending on preference, you can drizzle a little natural maple syrup over the oats and nuts for added flavor, if desired.

Melt peanut butter and Nutella in microwave and add to honey in a mixing bowl. Add oatmeal, and granola. When cool enough, combine remaining ingredients. Mix thoroughly. If after 5 minutes the mixture is too dry, add a little peanut butter and continue to mix. If it is too wet, add some more oats (They do not need to be toasted). The consistency should be like pottery clay, sticky to the touch, but not falling apart wet.

Freeze 20 minutes and enjoy! Keep cool in the fridge after that.

· · · · ·

This recipe was created by my nephew, Rob Breen. He knew of my love for peanut butter and had a sample waiting for me when we celebrated the Criss Christmas! I love it!

PEANUT BUTTER
RAISIN DIP

. . . . .

⅔ Cup creamy peanut butter
3 Tablespoons honey
Crackers of choice

⅔ Cup milk
⅓ Cup seedless raisins,
    chopped

In a small bowl, with electric mixer at medium speed, beat peanut butter, milk and honey until well blended. Stir in raisins. Cover; chill until serving time. Garnish with chopped peanuts, if desired. Great cracker dip!

. . . . .

I modified this recipe from one found on a box of my favorite crackers. It can also be used as a dip for apples!

BACON WRAPPED PEANUT BUTTER STUFFED JALAPENOS

. . . . .

8 jalapenos, halved lengthwise
and seeded

8 strips of bacon
½ Cup peanut butter

Fill each jalapeno with peanut butter and wrap with a half slice of bacon. Secure with a toothpick. Place jalapenos on a baking sheet and bake at 350 degrees for approximately 25 minutes or until bacon is browned.

. . . . .

While visiting a friend, Bob McDevitt, he told us about trying bacon wrapped jalapeno peppers stuffed with peanut butter. A great combination!

PROTEIN SNACKS

. . . . .

1 Cup peanut butter   ¼ Cup sesame seeds
½ Cup raisins   ¼ Cup honey
½ Cup nonfat dry milk

Mix together. Roll in 1-inch balls. Refrigerate.

Makes about 8 balls.

. . . . .

Variation: Substitution-Shaklee's Vanilla Protein for the nonfat dry milk.

This recipe came from a cookbook made by the staff and friends of Polyclinic Medical Center called "Recipes from our Hearts."

SOUPS

AFRICAN-PEANUT SOUP

. . . . .

1 onion, chopped
1 red bell pepper, chopped
2 Tablespoons peanut oil
4 Cups of chicken stock
Hot pepper flakes, to taste
1 Cup cooked, diced chicken
Salt and pepper to taste

1 green bell pepper, chopped
2 cloves garlic, chopped fine
1 (28 ounce) can stewed
   tomatoes, pureed
¼ Cup long grain rice
3 Tablespoons peanut butter
Chopped peanuts for garnish

In a large soup pot, warm the peanut oil over medium heat and add onion, peppers and garlic. Saute until the onion begins to brown. Add pureed tomatoes, chicken stock and hot pepper flakes, and simmer uncovered for 30 minutes. Add rice, chicken and peanut butter. Continue cooking another 10 to 15 minutes until the rice is done. Season with salt and pepper to taste.

. . . . .

Another recipe given to me by my friend, Susanne Ryan. The recipe appeared to be taken from a magazine, but the name of the magazine was unidentified.

PEANUT-Y SOUP

· · · · ·

2 Tablespoons butter or margarine
½ Cup chopped celery
3 Vegetable bouillon cubes
1½ teaspoons lemon juice

¼ Cup chopped onion
1 Cup peanut butter
4 Cups boiling water
Watercress

Melt butter in saucepan; add onion and celery. Cook until tender. Blend in peanut butter. Dissolve bouillon cubes in boiling water; add gradually to peanut butter mixture, blending well. Stir in lemon juice; heat to serving temperature. Garnish with watercress.

6 Servings.

· · · · ·

This recipe was borrowed from a women's club fundraising cookbook.

SWEET POTATO-PEANUT SOUP

· · · · ·

2 Tablespoons olive oil
¾ teaspoon salt
3 garlic cloves, finely chopped
2 teaspoons ground cumin
¼ teaspoon cayenne
14 ounce can crushed tomatoes
⅔ Cup creamy peanut butter
4 Cups water
Cilantro

1 large onion, chopped
½ teaspoon pepper
2 tablespoons ginger,
    freshly grated
1½ pounds sweet potatoes
    (about 2 large) peeled
    and cut into ½" pieces
Roasted peanuts, chopped

Heat olive oil in a large saucepan over medium heat. Add onion, season with salt and pepper and cook, stirring occasionally, until tender, 8 to 10 minutes. Stir in garlic and ginger and cook, stirring for 1 minute. Stir in cumin and cayenne and cook 1 more minute. Add sweet potatoes. Stir in tomatoes, peanut butter and water and bring to a boil. Reduce heat and simmer, covered until the sweet potatoes are tender, 18 to 20 minutes. Serve with cilantro and roasted peanuts, if desired.

· · · · ·

This recipe was modified from a collection of Fall favorites! Try it, you'll like it!

SALADS

APPLE RAISIN SALAD

· · · · ·

6 apples   1 Cup raisins
¼ Cup mayonnaise   ¼ Cup peanut butter
Walnuts or pecans, optional

Peel, core and dice apples. Mix with raisins. Combine peanut butter and mayonnaise. Pour over apples and raisins and mix well. Add nuts, if desired.

· · · · ·

This is one of my mother's all time favorite recipes and modified, by me, with the addition of peanut butter!

ROASTED SQUASH
AND KALE SALAD

· · · · ·

1 butternut squash, cut
   into 1-inch cubes
3 Tablespoons brown sugar
⅛ teaspoon pepper
1 peeled, julienned cucumber
2 teaspoons low sodium soy sauce
2 teaspoons sesame oil
2 Tablespoons creamy
   peanut butter

1 Tablespoon water
2 Tablespoons olive oil
½ teaspoon salt
1 pound thinly sliced kale
¼ Cup thinly sliced red
   onion
1 Tablespoon fresh lime juice
1 teaspoon sugar
2 teaspoons fresh ginger

Preheat oven to 400 degrees. Toss butternut squash with olive oil, brown sugar, salt and pepper. Bake for 25 minutes. Remove from oven and cool. Toss with kale, cucumber and red onion. In a blender, puree soy sauce, lime juice, sesame oil, sugar, peanut butter, ginger and water. Drizzle salad with dressing.

· · · · ·

It may take courage to try this recipe! Peanut butter in a salad combined with the leafy green, kale, could be the beginning of a new relationship. Even if you have never tasted kale, this recipe is worth a try!

MAIN DISHES

NUTTY NOODLES

. . . . .

4 to 5 Tablespoons peanut butter

3 teaspoons soy sauce

1 Tablespoon toasted sesame seeds

1 Tablespoon water

4 to 5 Cups cooked spaghetti
   noodles

Juice of 1 lemon

3 teaspoons peanut oil,
   (optional)

1 scant Cup finely chopped
   cucumbers, scallions,
   peppers, or carrots, or a
   mixture

Whisk together the first 6 ingredients in a bowl, or whirl in a blender. Add any combination of chopped vegetables, keeping the total quantity of vegetables less than a cup. Pour over the cooked noodles and mix well to distribute sauce evenly. Serve cold.

Makes 4 to 6 servings.

. . . . .

Source unknown.

SA-TEH
PEANUT BUTTER SAUCE

. . . . .

¼ Cup oil
1 onion, chopped
3 kaffir lime leaves
½ teaspoon curry powder
1 Cup coconut milk
½ Cup milk
3 bay leaves
1 to 3 Tablespoons fish sauce
(personal taste)
3 Tablespoons lemon juice

2 cloves garlic, minced
1 teaspoon ground dried red
chili peppers
1 Tablespoon chopped fresh
lemon grass
1 (2" piece) cinnamon stick
2 teaspoons tamarind paste
3 Tablespoons dark brown
sugar
1 Cup chunky peanut butter

Heat oil in a skillet to medium-high heat and saute garlic,
onion, chili peppers, kaffir lime leaves, curry powder and lemon
grass for 2 to 3 minutes. Stir in coconut milk, milk, cinnamon
stick, bay leaves, tamarind sauce, fish sauce, brown sugar, lemon
juice and peanut butter; mix well. Reduce heat and cook,
stirring frequently, until sauce thickens, about 30 minutes. Be
very careful sauce does not stick to bottom of pan.

. . . . .

*We went on a sailing trip to the British Virgin Islands with 4 other
couples and our friend, John Corcoran, did a lot of the cooking. One
of his specialties is SA-TEH PEANUT BUTTER SAUCE which*

(continued)

can be used as a dipping sauce for chicken, beef and pork which has been skewered and grilled. He provided us with a recipe book of the wonderful meals he made. This recipe is for the more adventurous cook, willing to seek out ingredients not normally found at the grocery store. I love this sauce, but I would rather just go to John's house and have him serve it or go on another sailing trip and let him be our chef! John is also a professional photographer and has captured the beauty of many lovely flowers. His work can be seen on his website at johncorcoranphotography.com.

SESAME NOODLES

. . . . .

2 Tablespoons canola oil
½ teaspoon dark sesame oil
1 teaspoon honey
3 Tablespoons peanut butter
6 ounces thin, whole wheat
    spaghetti
½ teaspoon crushed red pepper

2 garlic cloves, minced
2 teaspoons soy sauce
2 Tablespoons rice wine
    vinegar
¼ Cup boiling water
⅓ Cup thinly sliced
    scallions

Heat canola oil in a skillet over low heat. Add garlic cloves and cook until fragrant. Add dark sesame oil, soy sauce, honey, rice wine vinegar, peanut butter and boiling water. Stir constantly until thick and hot. Cook spaghetti according to package directions. Toss pasta and sauce together. Top with scallions and crushed red pepper.

. . . . .

It was an adventure branching out to main dishes using peanut butter, when most of my life "sweets" were the way to go for me. My tastes have broadened though, to include salads and main dishes, and I encourage others to do the same.

CAKES

CHIPS OF CHOCOLATE PEANUT BUTTER CAKE

· · · · ·

2¼ Cups flour
2 Cups brown sugar
1 Cup peanut butter
½ Cup butter or margarine
1 teaspoon vanilla

1 teaspoon baking soda
½ teaspoon baking powder
1 Cup milk
3 eggs
1 (12 oz.) package semi-
    sweet chocolate chips

In a large mixer bowl, combine flour, brown sugar, peanut butter and butter. Blend at low speed until crumbly. Reserve 1 Cup of this mixture. Add to the remaining crumb mixture the baking soda, baking powder, milk, eggs and vanilla. Mix until well blended (Batter will be slightly lumpy). Pour this batter into a well greased 13 × 9-inch cake pan. Sprinkle with the reserved crumbs. Sprinkle the chocolate chips over the crumb mixture. Bake at 350 degrees for 35 to 40 minutes or until a toothpick inserted in the center comes out clean.

· · · · ·

Variation: This recipe could be made with peanut butter chips if someone is unable to eat chocolate or a combination of both.

*This recipe was included in a gift from my good friend, Connie Hannah. It has become a **FAVORITE** of many of my friends and family! And me too!*

DELICIOUS DARK CHOCOLATE CAKE WITH PEANUT BUTTER FROSTING

· · · · ·

CAKE

2 Cups flour

1 teaspoon baking powder

½ Cup unsweetened cocoa

½ Cup vegetable oil

1 Cup buttermilk

1 teaspoon vanilla

1 teaspoon salt

2 teaspoons baking soda

2 Cups sugar

1 Cup hot prepared coffee

2 eggs

FROSTING

⅔ Cup butter or margarine

4 Cups powdered sugar

½ Cup peanut butter

¼ Cup milk

To prepare cake: Sift together all dry ingredients, including sugar, in a large mixing bowl. Add vegetable oil, coffee and milk and mix at medium speed for 2 minutes. Add eggs and vanilla and beat 2 more minutes (This batter will be thin). Pour in to a greased 9 × 13-inch pan. Bake at 325 degrees for 30 to 35 minutes.

To prepare frosting: Cream together butter and peanut butter. Gradually add powdered sugar and milk. Beat until smooth and nice spreading consistency. If frosting is too stiff, add more milk, 1 teaspoon at a time. Let cake cool before spreading with frosting.

· · · · ·

Another recipe from my days at Polyclinic Medical Center. Many meetings and luncheons resulted in additional peanut butter recipes for my collection and for that I am grateful!

JIMMY CARTER'S PEANUT BUTTER CAKE

. . . . .

1ST LAYER

1 Cup flour   ¼ pound (1 stick) butter
⅔ Cup chopped dry peanuts

Mix and press into 13 × 9-inch pan. Chill.

2ND LAYER

8 ounce cream cheese   ⅓ Cup peanut butter
1 Cup powdered sugar

Cream together and fold in 1 (8 ounce) container Cool Whip.

3RD LAYER

2 and ¾ Cups milk   1 box instant vanilla pudding
1 box instant chocolate pudding

Mix together milk and pudding.

4TH LAYER

1 (8 ounce) container Cool Whip

Top cake with Cool Whip.

To decorate, grate Hershey Bar and sprinkle with chopped peanuts.

. . . . .

This recipe was found in a local newspaper.

JOHN'S SECRET
PEANUT BUTTER CAKE

· · · · ·

CAKE

1 package Betty Crocker Super
    Moist Yellow Cake Mix
1⅓ Cups water
1 teaspoon vanilla

½ Cup Reese's Peanut
    Butter
⅓ Cup oil
3 large eggs

Mix the ingredients in a large bowl. Beat with electric mixer
until smooth. Pour into a 9 × 13-inch pan. Bake at 350 degrees
for 30 minutes or until toothpick inserted in center comes out
clean.

FROSTING

½ stick butter, softened
2 teaspoons vanilla
4 Cups powdered sugar

½ Cup Reese's Peanut
    Butter
½ Cup warm milk

Mix the butter, peanut butter, and vanilla in a large bowl. Beat
with electric mixer, slowly adding the warm milk. Add the
powdered sugar one cup at a time. Beat until smooth. Frost
cooled cake. Top with crushed peanut butter cups.

Tip: If you need to thin, add more milk. To stiffen, add more
powdered sugar. I often add more peanut butter to enhance the
peanut butter flavor!

(continued)

TOPPING
10 Reese's Peanut Butter Cups, crushed

Note: Freeze the peanut butter cups before hand. It makes the
job of crushing them much easier! I put them in a zipper-style
bag and crush with a hammer.

. . . . .

*I'll never forget the day my co-worker, John Carroll, made this cake
and brought it in for my birthday! It is the "Peanut Butter Lover's
dream come true!" I can only give credit to John as the source is
unknown, but it has become a favorite of many of my peanut butter
lovin' friends and family. My all time **FAVORITE!***

PEANUT BUTTER FUDGE CAKE

· · · · ·

CAKE

1 box Devil's Food Cake Mix

1 Cup buttermilk

2 Cups chopped chocolate covered peanut butter cups (about 8 ounces), plus more to garnish

1 Cup heavy cream

3 eggs

½ Cup vegetable oil

8 ounces dark chocolate, chopped

½ Cup peanut butter

Heat oven to 350 degrees. Coat two 9-inch round cake pans with nonstick cooking spray. Line with waxed paper; coat paper. In a large bowl, beat cake mix, eggs, buttermilk and vegetable oil on low for 30 seconds. Increase speed to medium-high; beat for 2 minutes, scraping down side of the bowl after 1 minute. Fold in 2 Cups of the chopped peanut butter cups.

Divide batter between prepared pans. Bake at 350 degrees for 34 minutes, or until a toothpick inserted in the center comes out clean. Let layers cool on a wire rack for 15 minutes. Turn out cakes onto wire racks to cool completely.

FROSTING

Place chopped dark chocolate in a medium-size bowl. Bring cream just to a boil and pour over chocolate. Whisk until chocolate melts. Add peanut butter and whisk until smooth.

(continued)

Trim top of cake layers flat with a serrated knife. Put 1 cake layer on cooling rack and place on a baking sheet. Pour 1 cup frosting on top; spread evenly with a spatula. Top with remaining cake layer. Pour remaining frosting over the top, allowing it to spill over the sides. Smooth top and sides with spatula. Refrigerate 1 hour to set. Transfer cake to serving plate and garnish with chopped candy, if desired.

· · · · ·

My friend, Susanne Ryan, gave me this recipe inside a little note offering to be the "food taster." The recipe appears to have come from a magazine, but it was not identified. When I made this cake, I gave a piece to Susanne and two other friends, Marlene and Pat. Although Marlene said she would savor it slowly throughout the week, she sent me an e-mail in about 2 days to say that it was delicious and all gone!

PEANUT BUTTER SURPRISE CUPCAKES

· · · · ·

CAKE

1 box chocolate cake mix

1 Cup powdered sugar

1 Cup peanut butter

2-3 Tablespoons milk

Mix and bake cupcakes as directed on box. While cupcakes are cooling, mix peanut butter, powdered sugar and milk together. After mixing well, place in a piping bag and insert into the middle of the cooled cupcakes.

FROSTING

¼ pound butter, (1 stick)

2½ Tablespoons flour

1 teaspoon vanilla

½ Cup cocoa

1½ Cups milk

1 box powdered sugar

Melt butter. Add cocoa and flour. Mix thoroughly and then add milk. Cook, stirring until thickened. Add vanilla and cool thoroughly. Add mixture to powdered sugar. Now spread on your cupcakes and enjoy!

· · · · ·

While staying at Eight Gables Inn in Gatlinburg, Tennessee, we were presented with dessert on a tray every evening, after we came in from having dinner. This was by far my favorite, but the others

(continued)

were delicious too! When I asked if I could include Peanut Butter Surprise Cupcakes in my future cookbook, they willingly obliged and even said they wanted to purchase one!

I cannot say enough good things about Eight Gables Inn. It is a wonderful Bed & Breakfast that serves outstanding breakfasts, has 17 candy dishes on a buffet to be enjoyed at any time, and the staff is fantastic. If you are planning a trip to Gatlinburg, this is the place to stay!

PEANUT BUTTER SWIRL
ICE CREAM CAKE

. . . . .

3 pints vanilla ice cream
4 TBSP butter, melted
25 Chocolate dipped wafer cookies
¼ Cup honey
½ Cup bottled hot fudge sauce

20 cream-filled chocolate
sandwich cookies
½ Cup peanut butter
(not reduced fat)
2 Tablespoons vegetable oil

Remove ice cream from freezer 30 minutes before using. Place chocolate sandwich cookies in food processor. Blend until crumbled. Add butter and blend again.

Stand wafer cookies along inside edge of 8-inch spring form pan. Set aside 2/3 Cup of chocolate crumb mixture. Spoon remaining crumb mixture into pan; press evenly over bottom.

Stir peanut butter, honey, and oil in small dish until well blended. Place softened ice cream in large bowl. Slowly pour about half of peanut butter mixture onto ice cream; Swirl together using a plastic spatula.

Spoon half of the ice cream mixture into the prepared pan; spread level. Sprinkle evenly with remaining chocolate crumb mixture, pressing mixture down with spoon.

(continued)

Spoon on remaining ice cream; spread level. Place the cake on cookie sheet and place in freezer. Freeze until cake is solid, at least 6 hours or over night.

To serve, stir fudge sauce in jar to loosen, but do not warm. Spoon remaining peanut butter mixture over top of cake along with spoonfuls of fudge topping. Swirl together. Let stand 10 minutes. Slice cake in to wedges.

. . . . .

This recipe was modified from a collection of cool treats for a warm summer day!

PEANUT BUTTER
TANDY CAKES

· · · · ·

4 eggs   1 teaspoon vanilla
2 Cups sugar   1 Tablespoon oil

Beat well.

Add ingredients below together and beat well with above
ingredients:

2 Cups flour   2 teaspoons baking powder
1 Cup milk   dash of salt

Place in a large greased cookie sheet with sides or a long cake
pan. Bake at 350 degrees for 25 minutes. Spread peanut butter
on cake while hot. Then cool in refrigerator.

Melt 1 8 oz. Hershey Chocolate Bar or (1 Cup dark chocolate
chips) with 1 Tablespoon of oil. Spread on cooled cake and
refrigerate. Cut into squares. (Make sure cookie sheet doesn't bend.)

Makes 20-30 pieces.

· · · · ·

*Another recipe from my days in hospital work. Osee was a nurse
from the old school who still wore a nurses cap. She brought this
cake to a luncheon which reminded everyone of Tasty Kake Tandy
Kakes. It's delicious! You'll want more!*

PEANUT CREAM-FILLED
"PERFECTLY CHOCOLATE" CHOCOLATE CAKE

· · · · ·

2 Cups sugar
1 ¾ Cups all-purpose flour
¾ Cup cocoa
1½ teaspoons baking powder
1½ teaspoons baking soda
1 teaspoon salt

2 eggs
1 Cup milk
½ Cup vegetable oil
2 teaspoon vanilla
1 Cup boiling water

Heat oven to 350 degrees. Grease and flour two 9-inch round pans. Combine dry ingredients in large bowl. Add eggs, milk, oil and vanilla. Beat 2 minutes on medium speed. Stir in boiling water (batter will be thin). Pour into pans. Bake 30 to 35 minutes. Cool 10 minutes; remove to wire racks. Spread half of Peanut Butter Cream between layers, remainder on top. Refrigerate 30 minutes. Drizzle with glaze. Store covered in refrigerator.

12 servings

PEANUT BUTTER CREAM

2 Cups whipping cream, divided

1 package (10 ounce) peanut butter chips

Cook ½ Cup whipping cream and 1 package (10 ounce) peanut butter chips over low heat, stirring constantly until smooth. Cool to room temperature. Beat 1½ Cups whipping cream until stiff. Stir ⅓ Cup into mixture. Fold in remainder. About 3½ cups.

COCOA GLAZE

3 Tablespoons butter
3 Tablespoons water
¼ teaspoon vanilla

3 Tablespoons cocoa
1 Cup powdered sugar

Melt butter, add cocoa and water, stirring until thickened. Remove from heat. Gradually add powdered sugar, whisk until smooth. Stir in ¼ teaspoon vanilla.

. . . . .

You will WOW your guests with this delicious peanut butter and chocolate combination! Source unknown.

SUE'S CAROB CAKE WITH PEANUT BUTTER ICING

. . . . .

½ Cup margarine
1 Cup brown sugar
1 Cup sugar
2 eggs
½ Cup carob (or cocoa)

½ Cup buttermilk
2 teaspoons vanilla
2 Cups flour
½ teaspoon salt
2 teaspoons baking soda,
in 1 Cup boiling water

Cream margarine and sugars, add eggs and vanilla. Cream well. Add carob (or cocoa). Sift flour and salt together. Add flour mixture and buttermilk alternately, mixing well. Add water/baking soda mixture, mix well. Pour into either 2 round cake pans or a 13 × 9 × 2-inch pan. Bake 350 degrees for 30 to 35 minutes.

Substitution: If you don't have buttermilk, add 1 Tablespoon vinegar to ½ cup milk.

PEANUT BUTTER ICING
6 Tablespoons butter
1 and ½ teaspoons vanilla

1 16 oz. bag of powdered sugar
1 Cup peanut butter

Cream butter and peanut butter. Add vanilla, add sugar with enough milk to get the consistency you want.

. . . . .

*If you can't eat chocolate, this is the cake for you. It is made with carob, but takes just like chocolate. Sue Romberger's cake has always been a hit at our Sunday School Class Picnics. I think because of the icing! You can't help but want to scrape your finger along the side of the pan to indulge in the icing! Although I love most of the recipes in this cookbook, this is another all time **FAVORITE**!*

CHEESECAKES

MINI PEANUT BUTTER CHEESECAKES

. . . . .

9-10 ounces chocolate cookies
   with peanut butter filling
1¼ Cups sugar
1 teaspoon vanilla extract
Chocolate Glaze (below)

2 (8 oz. each) cream cheese
1 Cup creamy peanut butter
3 large eggs, at room
   temperature

Heat oven to 325 degrees. Line muffin pans with 24 paper (not foil) baking cups. Break cookies into a food processor. Pulse until fine, moist crumbs form. Press about 1 Tablespoon evenly over bottom of each cup. Freeze until ready to fill. Beat next 4 ingredients in a large bowl with mixer on medium speed until smooth. On low speed, beat in eggs, one at a time, just until blended. Spoon about 2½ Tablespoons into each cup. Bake 20 minutes or until puffed. Some cracks may appear on top; that's OK. Cool completely in pans on a wire rack.

CHOCOLATE GLAZE

Meanwhile prepare Chocolate Glaze:

3 oz. semi-sweet baking chocolate
2 TBSP light corn syrup

2 TBSP unsalted butter
½ teaspoon vanilla extract

Microwave ingredients on medium stirring until smooth. Cool slightly. Peel off liners. Place cakes on a foil-lined baking sheet.

Spoon glaze over tops; sprinkle with nuts. Refrigerate for at least 2 hours for glaze to set.

Makes 24.

. . . . .

Variation: Substitution of low fat cream cheese can be used instead of regular cream cheese.

One of the many recipes I saved over the years and enjoyed serving to company. A small, but delightful treat!

PEANUT BUTTER
CHOCOLATE CHIP CHEESECAKE
· · · · ·

1¼ Cups graham cracker crumbs
¼ Cup cocoa
3 (8 ounce each) cream cheese, softened
1 (10 ounce) package peanut butter chips, melted
2 teaspoons vanilla

⅓ Cup sugar
⅓ Cup butter or margarine, melted
1 can (14 ounce) sweetened condensed milk
4 eggs
1 Cup semi-sweet chocolate chips, mini

Heat oven to 300 degrees. Stir together graham cracker crumbs, sugar, cocoa and butter. Press onto bottom of 9-inch spring form pan. In large mixer bowl, beat cream cheese until fluffy. Gradually beat in sweetened condensed milk, then peanut butter chips until smooth. Add eggs and vanilla; beat well. Stir in mini chocolate chips. Pour over crust. Bake 55 to 65 minutes or until center is set. Cool. Refrigerate. Garnish as desired. Cover; refrigerate leftover cheesecake.

12 Servings.

· · · · ·

"To die for" describes this outstanding peanut butter chocolate combination! A recipe found in the Sunday Paper many years ago.

PEANUT BUTTER CUP CHEESECAKE

· · · · ·

BROWNIE CRUST

1 Cup semi-sweet chocolate chips

6 Peanut butter cups
   cut into quarters

6 Tablespoons unsalted butter,
   melted

1 Tablespoon vanilla

1 Cup plus 2 Tablespoons flour

½ teaspoon baking powder

1 Cup peanut butter chips

1¼ Cups sugar

2 eggs

⅓ Cup unsweetened cocoa

½ teaspoon salt

CHEESECAKE FILLING

2 pounds cream cheese, softened

1½ Cups firmly packed
   brown sugar

½ Cup whipping cream

6 Peanut butter cups, cut into quarters

5 eggs at room temperature

1 Cup peanut butter

1 Tablespoon vanilla

GLAZE INGREDIENTS

8 ounces semi-sweet
   chocolate chips

2 Tablespoons light corn syrup

3 Tablespoons peanut butter

½ Cup whipping cream

FOR DECORATION

7 Peanut Butter Cups, cut in half

(continued)

Directions:

Heat oven to 350 degrees. Grease 9-inch spring form pan with butter.

Stir together melted butter, sugar and vanilla in a large bowl with spoon or wire whisk. Add eggs; stir until well blended. Stir in flour, cocoa, baking powder and salt; blend well. Spread in prepared pan.

Bake 25 to 30 minutes or until brownie begins to pull away from side of pan. Meanwhile, make cheesecake layer (see below).

Immediately after removing brownie from oven, sprinkle semi-sweet chocolate chips, peanut butter chips and peanut butter cups over brownie surface. Spoon cheesecake filling mixture over chips.

TURN OVEN DOWN TO 325 DEGREES.

CHEESECAKE FILLING

Beat cream cheese with electric mixer until smooth. Add eggs one at a time, beating well after each addition. Add sugar, peanut butter and cream; mix until smooth. Stir in vanilla. Pour filling into prepared crust.

Double-wrap spring form pan with aluminum foil to prevent water seeping in to the pan. Place spring form pan into a larger baking pan. Place hot water into the larger pan so that water comes 1 inch up the sides of the spring form pan. Bake at 325 degrees 1 and ½ hours, or until firm and lightly browned. Remove from the oven and allow to cool (approximately 1 hour).

Run a knife along the edge of the cake to loosen it from the pan. Refrigerate for at least 4 hours before decorating and then remove cake from pan and plate.

Glaze Directions:
In a double boiler or a bowl set over a pot of simmering water, melt the chocolate chips, peanut butter and corn syrup. When melted, remove from heat and whisk in the cream until it is a smooth, creamy consistency. Drizzle over cake and then add peanut butter cups around the edge of the cake.

· · · · ·

This is one of the best of my cheesecake recipes which includes an all time favorite, the peanut butter cup! Source unknown.

COOKIES

CRISS CROSS COOKIES

. . . . .

1 Cup natural peanut butter
½ Cup butter
½ Cup granulated sugar
½ Cup firmly packed brown sugar
3 Tablespoons water
¼ teaspoon salt

½ teaspoon vanilla
1 egg
1½ Cups flour
¾ teaspoon baking soda
½ teaspoon baking powder

Cream together peanut butter and butter. Add sugars gradually and cream together until light and fluffy. Add water, vanilla, and egg; beat well. Mix together flour, baking soda, baking powder, and salt; stir into peanut butter mixture. Shape into 1-inch balls and place about 2 inches apart on a cookie sheet. Flatten with a fork in a criss-cross pattern. Bake at 375 degrees for 10 to 12 minutes.

. . . . .

This recipe came from a newspaper insert. I had to include this one as it begins with my last name—CRISS! Source unknown.

DELICIOUS PEANUT BUTTER CHIP COOKIES

· · · · ·

1 box Pillsbury Plus Devil's Food
   Cake Mix
1 (10 oz.) package peanut
   butter chips

½ Cup oil
2 eggs

GLAZE
Reserved ½ Cup peanut
   butter chips

1 TBSP milk
2 TBSP margarine

Heat oven to 350 degrees. In large bowl, combine cake mix, oil and eggs. Mix well. Reserve ½ Cup peanut butter chips. Add remaining peanut butter chips to dough. Mix well. Drop by rounded teaspoon 2 inches apart on ungreased cookie sheet. Bake 9-12 minutes. Cool 2 minutes. Remove from cookie sheet. Cool completely.

In small saucepan, over low heat, melt all glaze ingredients, stirring constantly. Drizzle over cookies. Store between sheets of waxed paper in container.

· · · · ·

Source unknown.

GRANNIE'S
PEANUT BUTTER COOKIES

. . . . .

1 Cup butter or margarine
¾ Cup granulated sugar
1 Cup peanut butter, creamy or
    chunky
1 Cup bran
¾ Cup rolled oats

¾ Cup brown sugar
1 teaspoon vanilla
2 eggs, beaten
1¼ Cups all-purpose flour
2 teaspoons baking soda

Melt butter. Beat together with the sugars, vanilla, peanut butter and eggs. In a separate bowl, combine the flour, bran, oats and baking soda. Stir dry mixture into butter mixture. Drop by teaspoon onto ungreased cookie sheet. Bake at 350 degrees for 15 to 18 minutes. Let stand on cookie sheet for 1 minute before transferring to a wire rack to cool.

Makes 7 dozen.

. . . . .

This recipe came in a mailer and the source was unidentified.

ENTICING
PEANUT BUTTER COOKIES

· · · · ·

¾ Cup creamy peanut butter
1¼ Cups firmly packed light
  brown sugar
1 Tablespoon vanilla
1¾ Cups all purpose flour

¾ teaspoon baking soda
½ Crisco shortening
3 Tablespoons milk
1 egg
¾ teaspoon salt

Heat oven to 375 degrees. Combine peanut butter, Crisco, brown sugar, milk and vanilla in large bowl. Beat until well blended. Add egg and beat just until blended. Combine flour, salt and baking soda. Add to creamed mixture at low speed and mix just until blended. On ungreased baking sheet, drop by heaping teaspoonfuls 2 inches apart. Bake for 7 to 8 minutes, until just beginning to brown. Cool 2 minutes on baking sheet before removing to wire rack.

Makes 3 dozen.

· · · · ·

Variation: Flatten slightly in crisscross pattern with tines of fork.

Another delicious and "enticing" cookie recipe from the "peanut butter archives."

MOM'S COCONUT AND PEANUT BUTTER COOKIES

. . . . .

½ Cup butter or margarine, softened
1 Cup packed light brown sugar
1 egg
½ teaspoon vanilla
¾ teaspoon baking soda

1 Cup moist flaked or shredded coconut
½ Cup chunky peanut butter
½ teaspoon salt
1¼ Cups flour
⅜ teaspoon baking powder

In a large bowl, beat butter and peanut butter until blended. Add sugar; beat well. Beat in egg, salt and vanilla. Stir together flour, soda and baking powder. Stir into butter mixture until well blended. Stir in coconut. On lightly floured surface, shape in two (1 and ½ -inch each) diameter rolls; wrap in waxed paper; chill 2 hours or until firm. Slice 3/16 inch thick. Place 1 and ½ inches apart on greased baking sheets. Bake in 350 degree pre-heated oven 8 to 10 minutes or until golden brown. Remove to racks to cool.

. . . . .

Susanne Ryan provided this recipe, once again taken from a magazine, but no documentation as to which magazine. A very different combination of flavors, using peanut butter and coconut, these cookies are good with bananas or banana ice cream (according to the recipe). I, of course, would say, try it with peanut butter ice cream!

PB SANDWICH COOKIES

· · · · ·

1⅓ Cups flour
½ teaspoon salt
½ Cup packed light brown sugar
2 eggs
1 teaspoon vanilla
¼ Cup peanuts, finely chopped
1⅓ Cups marshmallow cream

½ teaspoon baking soda
½ Cup granulated sugar
⅓ Cup butter, at room temp
1 Tablespoon milk
1⅓ Cups chunky peanut
  butter

Heat oven to 375 degrees. Mix flour, baking soda and salt in a small bowl. Beat sugars and butter in medium-size bowl until well blended. Beat in eggs, milk, vanilla. On low speed, gradually beat in flour mixture. Stir in ⅔ Cup peanut butter. Drop by rounded teaspoonfuls onto ungreased baking sheet, 1 and ½ inches apart. Top each with ⅛ teaspoon chopped peanuts. Bake in 375 degree oven 8 to 10 minutes, until golden. Cool on wire racks. Spoon about 2 teaspoons marshmallow cream on flat side of half the cookies. Spread about 1 teaspoon peanut butter on flat side of remaining cookies. Sandwich cookies together.

Makes 30 cookies.

· · · · ·

Another of the 100 plus recipes resulting from my lifelong obsession with peanut butter!

QUICK PEANUT BLOSSOMS

. . . . .

1 (20 ounce) Package refrigerated peanut butter or sugar cookies	Sugar 36 Milk chocolate candy kisses

Heat oven to 375 degrees. Shape dough into 1-inch balls; roll in sugar. Place 2 inches apart on ungreased cookie sheets. Bake at 375 degrees for 10 to 12 minutes or until golden brown. Immediately top each cookie with a candy kiss, pressing down firmly so cookie cracks around edge; remove from cookie sheets. Cool completely.

Makes 3 dozen.

. . . . .

For the baker who wants to "Keep It Simple!" This recipe came in a small pamphlet in the newspaper called "EASY ENTERTAINING."

PEANUT BLOSSOMS

· · · · ·

Sift:

1¾ Cups flour

1 teaspoon baking soda

½ teaspoon salt

Cream:

½ Cup margarine

½ Cup peanut butter

½ Cup sugar

½ Cup brown sugar

Add:

1 unbeaten egg

2 Tablespoons milk

1 teaspoon vanilla

Blend in dry ingredients. Roll in sugar and place on ungreased baking sheets. Bake at 375 degrees for 8 minutes. Remove from oven and place a Hershey Kiss on top of each one, pressing down so that the cookie cracks around the edge. Put back in oven and bake 2 minutes longer. One large bag of kisses makes a double batch.

· · · · ·

My cousin, Joanie Bryner, gave me this recipe. She says, "It's foolproof!" And she mixes it by hand!

EASY PEANUT BUTTER COOKIES

. . . . .

1 (14 oz.) Can sweetened
   condensed milk
1 teaspoon vanilla extract
2 Cups Bisquick

¾ to 1 Cup peanut butter
1 egg (optional)
Granulated sugar

Preheat oven to 350 degrees. In a large bowl, beat peanut butter, sweetened condensed milk, egg and vanilla extract until smooth. Add Bisquick and mix well. Chill at least 1 hour. Shape into 1 inch balls, roll in sugar and place 2 inches apart on ungreased baking sheets. Flatten with fork. Bake 6-8 minutes or until lightly browned (Do not over bake).

Makes about 5 dozen.

. . . . .

My friend, Peggy Hartline, gave me this recipe. She does not like to bake, but this is an easy recipe she makes at Christmas and all her guests enjoy!

PEANUT BUTTER CUP
COOKIES

· · · · ·

½ Cup white sugar
½ Cup brown sugar
½ Cup butter or margarine
½ Cup peanut butter
1 egg

½ teaspoon vanilla
1¼ Cups flour
1 teaspoon baking soda
½ teaspoon salt
Mini peanut butter cups

Heat oven to 350 degrees. Cream together first 6 ingredients. Mix flour, salt, and baking soda together and add to first mixture. Roll dough into 36 one inch balls. Place in small muffin tins. After baking, remove from oven and immediately place mini peanut butter cup in center of each cookie. Let cool completely before removing from pans. Bake 8-10 minutes.

Makes 3 dozen.

· · · · ·

This cookie shows up at Church dinners, luncheons and at Christmas! They are always the first to go! Source unknown.

PEANUT BUTTER FINGERS #1

· · · · ·

1 package Fleishmann's active
   dry yeast
2 Tablespoons warm water
½ Cup granulated sugar
½ Cup packed brown sugar
1 egg
½ Cup creamy or super chunk
   peanut butter
Cocoa Glaze (below)

¼ Cup margarine or butter
   (softened)
¼ Cup shortening (Crisco)
1½ Cups Gold Medal
   All Purpose or Whole
   Wheat flour
¾ teaspoon baking soda
¼ teaspoon salt

Heat oven to 375 degrees. Dissolve yeast in warm water in large bowl. Mix in sugars, egg, peanut butter, margarine and shortening until smooth. Stir in flour, baking soda and salt. Cover and refrigerate 30 minutes. Shape dough by teaspoonfuls into 2 and 1/2 inch fingers on ungreased cookie sheet. Bake until light brown, about 8 minutes; cool. Dip one end of each cookie into Cocoa Glaze.

About 6 dozen cookies.

COCOA GLAZE
Mix 1 and ½ Cups powdered sugar and ¼ Cup cocoa in a medium bowl. Stir in 3 Tablespoons milk and 1 teaspoon vanilla until smooth. Stir in additional milk, ½ teaspoon at a time, until of desired consistency.

· · · · ·

Another recipe from my friend, Susanne Ryan, but I do not know the source.

PEANUT BUTTER FINGERS #2

· · · · ·

DOUGH

1 stick unsalted butter

½ Cup packed light brown sugar

1 large egg

½ teaspoon ground cinnamon

1½ Cups whole wheat flour

⅓ Cup English toffee bits

Toffee bits and peanuts
get mixed together

½ Cup chunky peanut butter

¼ Cup granulated sugar

½ teaspoon baking soda

1 Cup (6 ounces) semi-sweet
chocolate chips

⅓ Cup dry or honey-
roasted peanuts, coarsely
chopped

Heat oven to 325 degrees. Coat a 15 and ½ x 10 and ½-inch
jelly roll pan with nonstick spray. In a large bowl with mixer
on medium speed, beat butter, peanut butter, brown sugar,
granulated sugar, egg, baking soda and cinnamon until well
blended. Stir in flour just until blended. Press over bottom of
prepared pan; prick dough all over with a fork. Bake 15 to 18
minutes until golden. Sprinkle hot crust with chocolate chips,
let stand 5 minutes, then spread with a flexible spatula over
crust. With a toothpick, draw a line in chocolate to divide in
half crosswise, then divide each half in thirds (you'll have 6
rows). Sprinkle a 1¾-inch band of toffee-nut mixture down
scored lines 1, 3 and 5; press gently into chocolate. Then score
lengthwise to create 8 columns. While warm, cut through
scored lines with a sharp knife. Cool completely in pan. Remove
cookies with a long metal spatula.

(continued)

Tip: When cutting the cookies, wipe the knife blade clean between cuts.

Storage Tip: Store airtight at cool room temperature up to 1 week or freeze up to 1 month.

· · · · ·

This was part of an insert in a magazine with many different kinds of Christmas Cookies. Of course, I went right for the one with peanut butter!

PEANUT BUTTER PINWHEELS

. . . . .

½ Cup mashed potatoes
   (no salt or milk added)
4 Cups powdered sugar

1 Cup peanut butter
⅛ teaspoon salt
½ teaspoon vanilla

To the mashed potatoes, add salt and enough powdered sugar to make an easily handled fondant. Mix well. Add vanilla. Turn onto a surface lightly dusted with powdered sugar. Roll into a rectangular shape that is ½-inch thick. Spread with peanut butter. Roll up jellyroll fashion. Chill overnight. Cut into ¼-inch slices.

Makes about 4 dozen.

. . . . .

This recipe was given to me by my friend Susanne Ryan and clipped from a local newspaper.

CHEWY CHOCOLATE COOKIES

. . . . .

2 Cups all-purpose flour
¾ Cup cocoa
1 teaspoon baking soda
½ teaspoon salt
1¼ Cups (2½ sticks) butter or
    margarine, softened

2 Cups sugar
2 eggs
2 teaspoons vanilla extract
1 2/3 Cups (10 ounce
    package)
Reese's Peanut Butter Chips

Heat oven to 350 degrees. Stir together flour, cocoa, baking soda
and salt. In a large bowl, beat butter and sugar with an electric
mixer until light and fluffy. Add eggs and vanilla; beat well.
Gradually add flour mixture, beating well. Stir in peanut butter
chips. Drop by rounded teaspoons onto ungreased cookie sheet.
Bake 8 to 9 minutes (Do not over bake; cookies will be soft.
They will puff while baking and flatten while cooling). Cool
slightly; remove from cookie sheet to wire rack. Cool completely.

Makes 4½ dozen.

PAN RECIPE
Spread batter in greased 15½ × 10½ × 1-inch jelly roll pan.
Bake at 350 degrees for 20 minutes or until set. Cool completely
in pan on wire rack. Cut into bars.

. . . . .

Another recipe from a local newspaper insert.

BAR COOKIES

CHEWY PEANUT BUTTER
CARAMEL BARS

· · · · ·

1 package refrigerated
   sugar cookies
1 Cup light brown sugar, packed)
1 Cup granulated sugar
1 (12 ounce) bag milk chocolate
   baking chips
½ Cup finely chopped dry roasted peanuts

½ Cup butter
1 can (14 ounce) sweetened
   condensed milk
1¾ Cups graham cracker
   crumbs
½ Cup Jif Peanut Butter

Heat oven to 350 degrees. Spray 13x9-inch pan (dark pan not recommended) with non-stick cooking spray or line with non-stick foil. Evenly arrange cookie rounds in pan. Bake 24 to 26 minutes until lightly brown. Cool 15 minutes on cooling rack.

Meanwhile in 2 quart heavy saucepan, melt butter over medium heat. Stir in condensed milk, brown and granulated sugar until blended. Add graham cracker crumbs, mix well. Mixture will be thick. Bring to a boil, stirring constantly. Reduce heat to low, cook 5 minutes, stirring constantly or until slightly thickened. Pour caramel mixture over warm cookie crust, spreading evenly.

In medium bowl, microwave chocolate chips on high 1 minute to 1 minute 20 seconds, stirring every 30 seconds until smooth. Stir in peanut butter until blended. Spread evenly over caramel layer. Sprinkle with chopped peanuts. Refrigerate 1 hour or until chocolate is set. For bars, cut into 6 rows by 6 rows. Store covered in refrigerator.

· · · · ·

Variations: Chocolate chip refrigerated cookies can be used, and dark chocolate chips and a trail mix without the raisins instead of peanuts. "I also used the non-stick foil, so all you have to do is lift it out of the pan. You can use any ingredients and change it accordingly," as noted by Barb Byrem.

*I first tasted this recipe at a Church bake sale. They were made by Barb Byrem, a friend from Church, and I said, "I have to have that recipe!" She was very prompt in getting it to me and "bugged" me, no "encouraged" me to get working on the cookbook! These have been added to my **FAVORITE** list!*

CHOCOLATE PEANUT BUTTER CEREAL BARS

. . . . .

5 Cups Chocolate Cheerios Cereal
¾ Cup salted peanuts
½ Cup brown sugar, packed
1 Cup peanut butter

¾ Cup raisins
1 Cup corn syrup
½ cup granulated sugar
½ Cup milk chocolate chips

Spray 13 × 9-inch pan with cooking spray. In large bowl, combine cereal, raisins and peanuts; set aside. In 2 quart saucepan, combine corn syrup and sugars. Heat to boiling over medium heat, stirring constantly; remove from heat. Stir in peanut butter. Pour peanut butter mixture over cereal mixture; mix until thoroughly coated. Spread evenly in pan. In small microwave bowl, microwave chocolate chips on HIGH 1 minute, stirring every 15 seconds, until melted and smooth. Drizzle over bars. Refrigerate 15 minutes or until chocolate is set.

Tip: Place melted chocolate chips in a re-sealable plastic bag. Cut small piece off corner; drizzle chocolate over bars.

. . . . .

Source unknown.

CHOCOLATE PEANUT BUTTER SQUARES

· · · · ·

2 packages (10 ounces each) peanut butter chips
2 cans (14 ounces each) sweetened condensed milk
1 package (12 ounces) semi-sweet chocolate pieces
⅓ Cup butter or margarine
2 Cups finely ground graham-cracker crumbs
1½ Cups unsalted peanuts (finely chopped)

Line 13×9-inch baking pan with foil. Melt peanut butter chips and butter in a small saucepan until smooth. Spoon into large bowl. Whisk in sweetened condensed milk.

Gradually stir in crumbs and ½ Cup peanuts. (Use hands, if necessary, to mix thoroughly.) Pat the mixture evenly into the prepared pan. Refrigerate at least 30 minutes.

Melt chocolate pieces in small saucepan set over very low heat, stirring occasionally, until smooth. Spread over top of peanut mixture. Sprinkle with remaining peanuts. Set aside until firm. Cut into squares.

· · · · ·

This recipe was borrowed from an old magazine article and personalized by me!

DOUBLE DELICIOUS
COOKIE BARS

· · · · ·

½ Cup margarine or butter
1 (14 ounce) can sweetened
   condensed milk
1 Cup peanut butter chips

1½ Cups graham cracker
   crumbs
1 (12 ounce) package semi-
   sweet chocolate chips

Preheat oven to 350 degrees (325 for glass dish). In a 13×9-inch pan melt margarine in oven. Sprinkle crumbs evenly over margarine, stir and press into pan. Pour sweetened condensed milk evenly over crumbs. Top with chips; press down firmly. Bake 25 to 30 minutes or until lightly browned. Cool. Cut into bars. Store loosely covered at room temperature.

· · · · ·

These are a favorite! A recipe found in the Sunday paper coupon section.

GAME DAY
COOKIE BARS

· · · · ·

1½ Cups graham cracker crumbs
¼ Cup sugar
1 (14 ounce) can sweetened
   condensed milk
1 Cup peanut butter chips or
   butterscotch chips
1 (3½ ounce) can flaked coconut

¼ Cup cocoa
¼ Cup butter or margarine,
   melted
2 Cups (12 ounce) pkg. semi-
   sweet chocolate chips
1 Cup chopped nuts

Heat oven to 350 degrees (325 for glass dish). Combine crumbs, cocoa, sugar and margarine. Press firmly on bottom of 13×9-inch baking pan; pour sweetened condensed milk evenly over crust. Top evenly with remaining ingredients in the following order: semi-sweet chocolate chips, peanut butter chips (or butterscotch chips), coconut, nuts. Press down firmly. Bake 25 to 30 minutes or until lightly browned. Cool. Chill thoroughly if desired. Cut into bars. Store loosely covered at room temperature.

Makes 24 to 36 bars.

· · · · ·

Somewhat similar to Magic Bars, this recipe was in the Sunday paper.

MAGIC BARS

. . . . .

½ Cup butter, melted
1½ Cups graham cracker crumbs
1 (14 ounce) can Eagle Brand Sweetened Condensed Milk

2 Cups semi-sweet chocolate chips
1⅓ Cups flaked coconut
1 Cup chopped nuts

Heat oven to 350 degrees (325 for glass dish). Coat 13 × 9-inch baking pan with no-stick cooking spray. Combine graham cracker crumbs and butter. Press into bottom of prepared pan. Pour sweetened condensed milk evenly over crumb mixture. Layer evenly with chocolate chips, coconut and nuts. Press down firmly with a fork. Bake 25 minutes or until lightly browned. Cool. Cut into bars or diamonds.

Makes 36 bars.

Tip: I melt the butter in the oven as it pre-heats, but you must keep a close eye on it so it does not brown. Then I stir the graham cracker crumbs directly in to the pan.

. . . . .

Variations: White chocolate chips or substitute ¾ pound chocolate covered peanuts for semi-sweet chocolate chips and chopped nuts. Or check out Peanut Butter Cup Cookie Bars. They are delicious!

Where's the peanut butter?

I made adjustments to this old fashioned favorite! My husband cannot eat much chocolate, so when I make this recipe, I use one Cup chocolate chips on half the pan(for the chocolate lovers) and I use ½ Cup peanut butter chips and ½ Cup butterscotch chips on the other half. This is similar to the 7 Layer Cookie Bars which adds 1 Cup Butterscotch chips and 1 Cup semi-sweet chocolate chips or peanut butter chips. There are similar variations I have seen on the internet since I "invented" my creation, so I am not sure I should credit myself for this variation!

PEANUT BUTTER BARS

. . . . .

1 Cup Pillsbury's Best All Purpose Flour ½ Cup sugar
½ Cup firmly packed brown sugar ¼ teaspoon salt
½ teaspoon baking soda ½ Cup butter, softened
⅓ Cup creamy peanut butter 1 egg
½ teaspoon vanilla extract 1 cup quick cooking
1 cup semi-sweet chocolate pieces rolled oats

In large mixer bowl combine all ingredients except chocolate pieces. Blend with mixer until particles are course crumbs. Press in greased 9 × 13-inch pan.

Bake at 350 degrees for 20 to 25 minutes. Sprinkle immediately with chocolate pieces. Let stand 5 minutes. Spread evenly. Drizzle with Peanut Butter mixture. Cool. Cut into bars.

PEANUT BUTTER DRIZZLE
Combine ½ Cup confectioners' sugar, ¼ Cup creamy peanut butter and 2 to 4 Tablespoons milk. Mix well.

. . . . .

*Another Christmas **FAVORITE** of mine!! My friend JoAnn and her three sons would wait expectantly for the can of Christmas cookies I would give them each Christmas Eve. This was one of their favorites, too!*

PEANUT BUTTER BROWNIE
. . . . .

1 box of moist brownie mix
Tin foil cup cake papers

1 small bag peanut
butter cups

Mix brownie mix as directed on package. Line muffin pan with foil cups. Fill half full. Bake at 350 degrees for 7 minutes, then remove from oven. Remove paper from peanut butter cup and press in center of brownie. Finish baking for 6 more minutes.

. . . . .

This recipe was found in a local newspaper!

PEANUT BUTTER CUP COOKIE BARS

. . . . .

Crisco Original No-Stick
   Cooking Spray
2 Tablespoons peanut butter
1 (14 ounce) can sweetened
   condensed milk
1 Cup peanut butter chips
1⅓ Cups flaked coconut

1½ Cups graham cracker crumbs
3 Tablespoons powdered sugar
½ Cup butter, melted
¼ Cup peanut butter
1 Cup semi-sweet chocolate chips
1 Cup mini peanut butter cups
   or chopped up peanut
   butter cups

Heat oven to 350 degrees. Coat a 9 × 13-inch baking pan with no-stick cooking spray. In a food processor, combine graham cracker crumbs, powdered sugar and 2 Tablespoons peanut butter. Pulse to combine. Combine graham cracker crumb mixture and ½ Cup melted butter in a small bowl. Press into bottom of prepared pan.

Put ¼ Cup peanut butter into a bowl and microwave for approximately 15 seconds. Combine peanut butter with sweetened condensed milk and stir well to combine. Pour sweetened condensed milk/peanut butter mixture evenly over crumb mixture. Layer evenly with chocolate chips, peanut butter chips, peanut butter cups and coconut. Press down firmly. Bake 25 to 30 minutes or until lightly browned. Loosen from sides of pan while still warm; cool on wire rack.

. . . . .

Adapted from Eagle Brand Magic Cookie Bar Recipe. Actual source unknown.

PEANUT BUTTER
MARSHMALLOW BARS

· · · · ·

1 box chocolate cake mix
1 egg
1 Cup chocolate chips
1 can (14 ounce) sweetened
   condensed milk

½ Cup butter, melted
1 Cup peanut butter chips
1 Cup Jet Puff Marshmallow
   Bits

In a bowl, stir together cake mix, butter and egg. Mixture will be very thick. Line a 9 × 13-inch cake pan with foil and spray with non-stick cooking spray. Pat chocolate mixture into pan and top with chips and marshmallow bits. Drizzle with sweetened condensed milk. Bake at 350 degrees for 28 to 30 minutes. Remove from oven. Let cool 20 minutes and then put in fridge until ready to cut. Remove bars and foil from pan, peel back foil and cut.

· · · · ·

Adapted from the original Eagle Brand Magic Cookie Bar Recipe. Actual source unknown.

PEANUT BUTTER
AND FUDGE BROWNIES

· · · · ·

CHOCOLATE PORTION

2 Cups sugar

1 Cup butter or margarine, softened

1½ Cups All Purpose or
   Unbleached Flour

1 teaspoon baking powder

1 Cup peanut butter chips

4 eggs

2 teaspoons vanilla

¾ Cup unsweetened
   cocoa

½ teaspoon salt

PEANUT BUTTER PORTION

¾ Cup peanut butter

⅓ Cup butter or margarine, softened

¾ teaspoon vanilla

⅓ Cup sugar

2 Tablespoons flour

2 eggs

FROSTING

3 ounces unsweetened chocolate

2 and 2/3 Cups powdered sugar

¼ teaspoon salt

4 to 5 Tablespoons water

3 Tablespoons butter or
   margarine

¾ teaspoon vanilla

Heat oven to 350 degrees. Grease 13 × 9-inch pan. In large bowl, beat 2 cups sugar and 1 cup margarine until light and fluffy. Add 4 eggs, one at a time. Beat well after each addition. Add 2 teaspoons vanilla; blend well. Lightly spoon flour into measuring cup; level off. In small bowl, combine 1 and ½ Cups flour, cocoa, baking powder and ½ teaspoon salt. Gradually add flour mixture to sugar mixture; mix well. Stir in peanut butter chips.

In small bowl, beat peanut butter and ⅓ Cup butter until smooth. Add ⅓ cup sugar and 2 tablespoons flour; mix well. Add ¾ teaspoon vanilla and 2 eggs; blend well. Spread half of chocolate mixture in greased pan. Spread peanut butter mixture evenly over chocolate mixture. Spread remaining chocolate mixture evenly over peanut butter mixture. Pull knife through layers in wide curves, to marble.

Bake at 350 degrees for 40 to 50 minutes or until top springs back when touched lightly in center and brownies begin to pull away from sides of pan. Cool completely.

In medium saucepan over low heat, melt chocolate and 3 tablespoons butter, stirring constantly until smooth. Remove from heat. Stir in powdered sugar, ¼ teaspoon salt, ¾ teaspoon vanilla and enough water for desired spreading consistency. Frost cooled brownies. Cut into bars.

Makes 36 bars.

. . . . .

A new twist to an old recipe! Brownies with peanut butter!

PEANUT BUTTER AND FUDGE SWIRL BROWNIES

. . . . .

1 box Fudge Brownie Mix *
½ Cup water
¼ Cup vegetable oil
2 eggs
½ Cup Smucker's Natural
  Peanut Butter, Creamy

¾ Cup Smucker's Dove
Dark Chocolate Ice
Cream Topping
½ Cup Smucker's Caramel
  Topping

Heat oven to 350 degrees. Grease bottom of 9 x 13-inch pan.
Mix brownie mix, water, oil, eggs and Dark Dove Chocolate Ice
Cream Topping in a large bowl. Beat 50 strokes by hand until
all ingredients are well mixed. In a small bowl, mix the ½ Cup
Smucker's Caramel Topping and ½ Cup Smucker's Natural
Peanut Butter. Spread the brownie mixture in the greased
pan. Take the mixture of peanut butter and caramel topping
and drop spoonfuls over brownie mixture. With a knife, pull
through the pan creating a marbled effect. Bake 31-35 minutes.
Cool completely. Store covered.

Makes 20 brownies.

*USE A FAMILY SIZE BROWNIE MIX AS THIS RECIPE
CAME FROM A TIME WHEN BOXES OF BROWNIES
ALWAYS MADE A 9 × 13 PAN.

. . . . .

Taken from the Sunday Paper coupon section. Source unknown.

PEANUT BUTTER
RAISIN BARS

· · · · ·

½ Cup peanut butter
1½ Cups sugar
1 Tablespoon vanilla
1½ teaspoons baking powder
2 ounces (2 squares) semi-sweet
    baking chocolate

½ Cup butter or margarine
2 large eggs
1 Cup all-purpose flour
1½ Cups raisins

Combine peanut butter and butter; stir over medium-low heat until melted. Remove from heat; stir in sugar, eggs and vanilla. Combine flour and baking powder, stir into mixture. Stir in raisins. Spread batter in greased and floured 13 × 9-inch pan. Bake at 350 degrees for 25 minutes or until pick inserted in center comes out clean. Cool on wire rack. Place chocolate in small bowl. Microwave on High 3 to 4 minutes until melted, stirring every minute. Drizzle over top. Cool.

Makes 32 bars.

· · · · ·

Peanut Butter and Raisins. Not a combination you think of as quickly as Peanut Butter and Chocolate, but a combination that put this recipe on my husband's top 5 list. Give it a try and see what you think!

An advertisement in a national magazine.

PEANUT BUTTER
BLONDIES

. . . . .

⅔ Cup butter or margarine,
  softened
1 Cup packed light brown sugar
½ Cup granulated sugar
¾ Cup REESE'S Creamy
  or Crunchy Peanut Butter
2 eggs
1 teaspoon vanilla extract

⅓ Cup milk
1¾ Cups all-purpose flour
1 teaspoon baking powder
1⅓ Cups (10 ounce package)
  Reese's Peanut Butter
  Chips, divided)
Chocolate Brownie Frosting

Heat oven to 325 degrees. Grease 13 × 9 × 2-inch baking pan.

In a large bowl, beat butter, brown sugar, granulated sugar and peanut butter until creamy. Add eggs and vanilla; beat well. Gradually beat in milk. Gradually beat in flour and baking powder, beating thoroughly. Stir in 1 Cup peanut butter chips. Spread batter into prepared pan.

Bake 40 to 45 minutes or until wooden pick inserted in center comes out clean. Cool completely in pan on wire rack. Meanwhile, prepare Chocolate Brownie Frosting; spread over top of blondies. Sprinkle remaining ⅓ Cup peanut butter chips on top. Cut into bars.

About 36 bars.

. . . . .

*Another long, tedious meeting at the hospital saved by this delicious bar cookie! For anyone allergic to chocolate or if you don't like chocolate (how can that be!) this recipe can be made by omitting the icing and they are still a great treat! This recipe can be made with Peanut Butter Icing for the true peanut butter lover, who does not need chocolate for a fix! These are a **FAVORITE** of my husband and me! Source unknown.*

CHOCOLATE BROWNIE FROSTING

¼ Cup butter or margarine, softened 2 Tablespoons milk
¼ Cup Hershey's Cocoa   1½ Cups powdered sugar
1 Tablespoon light corn syrup   1 teaspoon vanilla extract

In medium bowl, beat butter, cocoa, corn syrup, milk, and vanilla until smooth. Gradually add powdered sugar, beating until spreading consistency.

About 1¼ Cups Frosting.

TOLL HOUSE
PEANUT BUTTER BROWNIES

· · · · ·

2½ Cups flour

2½ teaspoons baking powder

½ teaspoon salt

⅔ Cup butter

⅔ Cup peanut butter

1¼ Cups sugar

1¼ Cups brown sugar

1 teaspoon vanilla

3 eggs

1 (12 ounce) semi-sweet
    chocolate chips (divided)

Heat oven to 350 degrees. Combine flour, baking powder, and salt. Combine butter, peanut butter, sugar, brown sugar, and vanilla. Beat until creamy. Add eggs. Add flour mixture. Add 6 ounces chocolate chips. Spread in a well-greased 15 × 10 × 1-inch pan. Bake 35 minutes. Sprinkle remaining chocolate chips on top. Let stand 5 minutes. Spread evenly.

Makes 36.

· · · · ·

*My sister, Ellen Furlong, used to make this recipe when I went to visit. Another one of my **FAVORITES***!

CANDY

CHOCOLATE
PEANUT BUTTER CHIP FUDGE

. . . . .

2 Cups (12 ounce package)
   semi-sweet chocolate chips
1 teaspoon vanilla extract
1 Cup peanut butter chips

1 can (14 ounce) sweetened
   condensed milk
Dash salt

Line 8-inch square pan with foil. In heavy saucepan over low heat, melt chocolate chips with sweetened condensed milk, vanilla and salt; blend well. Remove from heat. Add peanut butter chips; stir just to distribute chips throughout mixture. Spread evenly into prepared pan. Refrigerate 2 hours or until firm. Remove from pan; peel off foil. Cut into squares. Store tightly covered in refrigerator.

. . . . .

An insert in the coupon section of a local newspaper. Actual source unknown.

CHOCOLATE
PEANUT BUTTER TRUFFLES
· · · · ·

1 package (8 squares) semi-
   sweet baking chocolate

½ Cup peanut butter
1 (8 ounce) Cool Whip (thawed)

Suggested coatings: powdered sugar, finely chopped pecans, toasted coconut, grated semi-sweet baking chocolate, finely crushed Nabisco Cookies, colored sprinkles.

Microwave chocolate in large bowl on HIGH for 2 minutes or until chocolate is almost melted, stirring after 1 minute. Stir until chocolate is completely melted.

Stir in peanut butter until well blended. Cool to room temperature. Gently stir in whipped topping. Refrigerate 1 hour.

Scoop truffle mixture with melon baller or teaspoon, then shape in to one inch balls. Roll in suggested coatings. Store in refrigerator.

Makes 3 dozen.

SUPER NUTTY CHOCOLATE TRUFFLES
Mix and refrigerate truffle mixture as directed, using chunky peanut butter. Shape into balls. Roll in finely chopped peanuts.

· · · · ·

This recipe was given to me by my friend Susanne Ryan, but I do not have documentation as to where she got the recipe.

CHOCOLATE-PEANUT BUTTER CRUNCH BALLS

. . . . .

1 Cup chunky peanut butter	½ Cup dark corn syrup
1 Cup crisp rice cereal	8 ounces milk chocolate,
¼ Cup finely chopped peanuts	broken in pieces

Beat peanut butter and corn syrup in medium-size bowl until well blended. Stir in cereal until well mixed. Using rounded teaspoon, shape mixture into balls. Place on aluminum foil-lined large baking sheet. Chill several hours or until firm. Place 6 ounces chocolate in medium-size bowl. Cover with plastic wrap. Microwave at full power for 1 minute. Stir chocolate until melted and smooth. Add the remaining chocolate and continue stirring until smooth and well blended. Using a fork, spear peanut butter balls; dip into chocolate, turning to coat completely; shake off excess chocolate by gently tapping fork on edge of bowl. Return to baking sheet. If chocolate thickens too much, microwave at 50% power for 30 seconds, until soft enough to dip. Let stand about 2 hours or until chocolate is almost firm. Sprinkle tops with finely chopped peanuts. Let stand until hardened.

. . . . .

This recipe was part of an insert in a national magazine.

DOUBLE DECKER MARBLED MELTAWAY FUDGE

· · · · ·

1½ Cups semi-sweet
   chocolate chips, divided
3½ Cups sugar
1 (12 ounce) can evaporated milk
½ Cup butter

2 Tablespoon light corn syrup
1 Tablespoon white vinegar
2½ Cups creamy or
   crunchy peanut butter
1 jar (7 oz.) marshmallow
   cream

Line 9 × 13-inch pan with foil. Place 1 cup chocolate chips in large heatproof bowl. In 4 quart saucepan, combine sugar, evaporated milk, butter, corn syrup and vinegar. Cook over medium heat, stirring constantly, until mixture comes to full rolling boil; boil and stir 5 minutes. Remove from heat. Add peanut butter and marshmallow cream; stir until smooth. Pour one half of peanut butter mixture over chocolate chips; stir until smooth. Pour chocolate mixture into prepared pan; top with remaining peanut butter mixture. Immediately sprinkle remaining ½ Cup chips over surface. With knife or metal spatula, gently swirl chips for marbled effect. Cool. Cut into squares. If a firmer fudge is desired, store covered in refrigerator. About 8 dozen pieces.

· · · · ·

Double Decker Delicious! Source unknown.

HEALTHY FUDGE

. . . . .

1 Cup honey
1 Cup peanut butter
1 Cup carob powder
1 Cup unhulled sesame seeds

1 Cup sunflower seeds, hulled
½ Cup shredded coconut
½ Cup chopped dates

Mix peanut butter and honey. Add carob, then remaining ingredients. Pour into oiled (Pam) 8 × 8-inch pan and refrigerate to harden. Cut in to squares.

Note: Try to cut down on honey each time you make it.

. . . . .

Who thought fudge could be healthy? This recipe was printed in *Recipes from our Hearts*, a cookbook prepared by Polyclinic Medical Center Staff.

HOMEMADE PEANUT BUTTER CUPS

· · · · ·

1 (11½ oz.) package milk
   chocolate chips, divided
1½ Cups confectioners' sugar
¼ Cup butter, softened

3 Tablespoons vegetable
   shortening, divided
1 Cup creamy peanut butter

Line a 12-cup muffin tin with paper baking cups. In a
small saucepan, melt 1 and ¼ cups chocolate chips and two
Tablespoons shortening over low heat, stirring just until
mixture is smooth. Allow to cool slightly; mixture should still
be pourable. Starting halfway up each paper cup, spoon about
2 teaspoons of mixture over inside of cups, completely covering
bottom half of each cup. Chill about 30 minutes or until firm.

In a large bowl, combine confectioners' sugar, peanut butter,
and butter; mix well (Mixture will be dry). Spoon evenly into
chocolate cups and press down firmly.

Place remaining chocolate chips and shortening in saucepan and
melt over low heat, stirring just until mixture is smooth. Spoon
equal amounts into cups, spreading to completely cover peanut
butter mixture. Cover and chill at least 2 hours, or until firm.

· · · · ·

I have made these and love them. Scrumptious! Source unknown.

PEANUT BUTTER EGGS

· · · · ·

FILLING

2 (8 ounce) packages cream cheese
4 pounds powdered sugar
Dash salt x 2

2 sticks (½ pound) butter
2 teaspoons vanilla
16 Tablespoons (heaping)
    peanut butter

Cream butter, cream cheese and peanut butter with hands until well mixed and smooth. Add vanilla and salt and mix well. Work in powdered sugar.

CHOCOLATE COATING

Melting chocolate (about 2 pounds)

Melt in top of double boiler. Dip with slotted spoon or large two pronged fork. Lay on waxed paper lined cookie sheet. Refrigerate.

Tip: Once you have formed the eggs, refrigerate briefly to make coating easier. This recipe is already doubled, so if you prefer making a single batch, just cut in half. You can adjust the peanut butter amount to your taste. The initial recipe called for 8 heaping Tablespoons, but it just wasn't enough peanut butter for this peanut butter lover!

· · · · ·

I used this recipe in a Cooking Class 30 plus years ago when I worked at Blue Ridge Haven East Nursing Home. We ate the

*peanut butter eggs, but made a cookbook, included this recipe
in it and sold it at a Fair/Bake Sale. I used it again at a Senior
Apartment Building (Presbyterian Apartments) where I worked and
we sold them at our annual bake sale. The head of our maintenance
department, John Carroll, assisted with coating the eggs. He went on
to make them for his family at Easter and it became a tradition that
he would not show up to Easter Dinner without his peanut butter
eggs! How could they not be a **FAVORITE** of mine?*

MICROWAVE
PEANUT BUTTER EGGS

· · · · ·

1¼ Cups graham cracker crumbs   1⅓ sticks margarine
2 Cups confectioners' sugar   1 Cup peanut butter
12-ounce chocolate chips or candy coating

In 1½ quart bowl or casserole, microwave margarine on HIGH for 1 to 2 minutes, until melted. Add crumbs, sugar, and peanut butter; mix well. Chill until firm. Shape into eggs and refrigerate. Microwave chocolate chips in covered casserole on MEDIUM for 6 to 8 minutes, stirring every two minutes, until completely melted. Using toothpicks, dip eggs into melted chocolate to coat. If chocolate starts to harden, reheat as at first. Chill eggs on cookie sheet until firm.

· · · · ·

Printed in a Newsletter from a job where I worked in the 90's. No documentation as to who submitted it.

PEANUT BUTTER
FUDGE

. . . . .

2 Cups sugar	2 Tablespoons molasses
1/2 Cup evaporated milk	(King Syrup)

Bring to a rolling boil and stir constantly for 3 minutes. Remove from heat and add these ingredients:

3 Tablespoons peanut butter	1 Tablespoon margarine
3 Tablespoons marshmallow cream	

Beat until smooth and pour into square buttered pan. Let cool. Empty onto a buttered piece of waxed paper, cut into pieces. If you double the recipe, double the cooking time.

. . . . .

*Recipe provided by Marie, a young woman with whom my mother used to work. I found the recipe on a small piece of paper in one of my mother's cookbooks. A **FAVORITE**? Yes!*

PRETZEL CANDY

. . . . .

1 (12 ounce) package white
   chocolate chip morsels
1 (10 ounce) package peanut butter
   chip morsels

1 Tablespoon peanut butter
1 Cup mixed nuts (or
   your favorite nuts)
1 Cup thin pretzels, broken

In a microwave safe dish, combine white chocolate chip morsels, peanut butter chip morsels, and peanut butter. Microwave on high for two minutes. Stir until blended. Add nuts and pretzels.

Line a baking sheet with foil. Spread mixture on foil lined cookie sheet. Once the candy has hardened, crack and enjoy!

. . . . .

My niece, Meg Breen, brought this to the Criss Christmas and everyone loved it! The Pretzel Candy was made by Meg's friend, Rosalyn Kirsopp. Thank you Rosalyn for sharing this delicious recipe!

NO BAKE RECIPES

CHOCOLATE PEANUT SWEETIES

. . . . .

1 Cup peanut butter
½ Cup butter (no substitutes)
3 Cups confectioners' sugar
5 dozen miniature pretzel twists
   (about 3 cups)

1½ Cups milk chocolate
   chips
1 Tablespoon vegetable oil

In a mixing bowl, beat peanut butter and butter until smooth. Beat in confectioners' sugar until combined. Shape into one inch balls; press one on each pretzel. Place on waxed paper-lined baking sheets. Refrigerate until peanut butter mixture is firm, about 1 hour. In a microwave-safe bowl or heavy saucepan, melt chocolate chips and oil. Dip the peanut butter ball into the chocolate. Return to baking sheet, pretzel side down. Refrigerate for at least 30 minutes before serving. Store in the refrigerator.

Yield: 5 dozen.

. . . . .

This recipe was clipped from an old recipe magazine.

EASY CANDY MAKING
FOR KIDS

· · · · ·

2 Cups powdered sugar   ¼ Cup peanut butter
4 Tablespoons milk   ½ Cup cocoa

Mix powdered sugar, milk, peanut butter and cocoa. Roll in balls and chill.

· · · · ·

Borrowed from "The Kitchen Cabinet," a handout with recipes for children.

PEANUT BUTTER
MUNCHIES

. . . . .

1 and ¼ Cups graham cracker
   crumbs
1 Cup peanut butter
½ Cup chopped walnuts

1 Cup unsifted
   confectioners' sugar
¼ Cup butter (softened)
½ Cup flaked coconut

Mix graham cracker crumbs, confectioners' sugar, peanut butter and butter in a medium bowl, using a wooden spoon. Roll between palms to shape into small balls. Roll half in nuts and half in coconut. Refrigerate.

Makes 2-3 dozen.

. . . . .

*When I walk in to my dad's house at Christmas, these are expected. They are also anticipated for his birthday! For that matter, he would eat them anytime! So would I. They are a **FAVORITE**! A great snack for a quick protein boost. My family members prefer the ones rolled in nuts best! Source unknown.*

PEANUT BUTTER OATIES

· · · · ·

2 Cups sugar
½ pound butter (2 sticks)
6 Tablespoons cocoa
½ Cup milk

¾ Cup peanut butter
1 teaspoon vanilla
3 Cups oatmeal

Mix sugar, butter, cocoa, and milk in saucepan and bring to a boil. Remove from heat. Add other ingredients and mix. Drop by spoonfuls on to waxed paper. Allow to set for several hours.

Makes 3 dozen.

· · · · ·

A recipe that has been around for many years and is still a favorite! This recipe could probably be found in just about any fundraising cookbook across the country.

PEANUT BUTTER
POPCORN BALLS #1

· · · · ·

½ Cup caramel syrup
½ Cup semi-sweet chocolate
   chips
4 Cups prepared plain popcorn

⅔ Cup reduced-fat or
   regular peanut butter
½ Cup chopped peanuts

Combine caramel syrup and peanut butter in a small bowl. Fold in chocolate chips and chopped nuts. Place popcorn in a large bowl. Pour caramel over top; mix with hands (mixture will be sticky). Using plastic wrap to prevent sticking, compress about 2 Tablespoons popcorn mixture into a 2-inch ball. Transfer to waxed paper. Continue with remaining mixture. Refrigerate if desired.

Makes 2 dozen.

· · · · ·

This recipe came from a national magazine.

PEANUT BUTTER
POPCORN BALLS #2

. . . . .

2 graham cracker squares
   (2 and ½ inch squares)
1 and ½ teaspoons granulated
   sugar
3 Tablespoons half-and-half

¼ Cup smooth peanut
   butter
½ teaspoon chocolate
   extract
2 Cups unsalted popped
   popcorn

Between 2 sheets of waxed paper, crush graham crackers with
a rolling pin; set aside. In small saucepan, over medium heat,
combine peanut butter, sugar and extract with 2-3 tablespoons
of half-and-half. In medium bowl, using wooden spoon,
combine popcorn and peanut butter mixture; form into 4 equal
balls. Roll balls in cracker crumbs, using all crumbs. Refrigerate
30 minutes before serving.

Makes 4 Servings.

. . . . .

This recipe came from a calorie conscious cookbook.

DESSERTS

CHOCOLATE PEANUT BUTTER DESSERT

· · · · ·

1 Devil's Food Cake Mix

¾ Cup creamy peanut butter

¼ pound butter (1 stick)

1 - 7 (oz.) jar marshmallow cream

Heat oven to 350 degrees. Mix cake mix and butter thoroughly. Reserve 1 cupful. Pat remaining mixture in an oiled 9 × 13-inch pan. Mix the peanut butter and marshmallow cream together and spread over cake mix. Crumble reserved cup of cake mix on top. Bake 15-20 minutes.

· · · · ·

Only four ingredients but WOW! Found on a recipe card (my handwriting) among my many recipes, but I do not know the source.

FRUIT
ROLL UPS

. . . . .

1 package (13⅓ ounces) 6 or
    7 inch flour tortillas
⅔ Cup fruit preserves (grape,
    peach, apricot, pineapple,
    cherry, strawberry)

1¼ Cups chunky peanut
    butter
Vegetable oil
Powdered sugar

Spread each tortilla with 2 tablespoons peanut butter. Spread
1 Tablespoon preserves across one end of each tortilla; roll up.
Heat oil (1 inch)) in 10- inch skillet to 350 degrees. Fry 3 or 4
roll-ups at a time, seam side down, until golden brown, turning
once, about 1½ minutes. Drain. Sprinkle with powdered sugar.

Makes 10 Fruit Roll Ups.

. . . . .

This is my modification to a popular Mexican dessert.

ICE BOX DESSERT

. . . . .

25-28 Oreo Cookies (crumbled)　　8 oz. cream cheese
2 Cups confectioners' sugar　　⅔ Cup peanut butter
1 Cup milk　　2 (8 oz.) containers of
½ to 1 Cup chopped walnuts　　　Cool Whip

In large mixing bowl combine cream cheese, sugar, peanut butter and milk. Whip together, then fold in both containers of Cool Whip. Put crumbled Oreo cookies in 9 × 13-inch cake pan. Pour mixture over cookies. Top with chopped nuts and freeze.

. . . . .

A recipe brought to a luncheon at one of my workplaces many years ago. Source not identified.

PEANUT BUTTER
BANANA CRUNCH

· · · · ·

4 Cups sliced bananas (6 medium)
1/2 teaspoon cinnamon
1/2 Cup brown sugar (packed)
1 Tablespoon butter or margarine

1 Tablespoon lemon juice
1/2 Cup flour
1/3 Cup chunky peanut
butter

Place bananas in 8" round baking dish. Add lemon juice and cinnamon, stirring lightly to coat fruit. In small bowl, combine flour and brown sugar. Cut in peanut butter and margarine until mixture is crumbly. Sprinkle over bananas. Bake in a 375 degree oven for 25 minutes.

Serves 6.

· · · · ·

Another recipe from Cooking Class at the Nursing Home where I worked. Peanut Butter and Banana has always been a great combination and teams up again for a great winner! Source unknown.

PEANUT BUTTER BROWNIE TRIFLE WITH BANANAS AND CARAMEL

· · · · ·

1 (17 to 20 ounce) package
   brownie mix, (plus required
   ingredients)
3 large bananas, sliced
6 Tablespoons unsalted roasted peanuts, roughly chopped

12 large peanut butter cups
1 Cup heavy cream
6 Tablespoons caramel sauce

Heat the oven according to brownie mix package directions. Lightly coat a 9-inch square pan with cooking spray. Line the pan with foil, leaving 3- inches folded over the two ends. Spray the foil.

Prepare the brownie batter according to package directions. Place half the batter in the pan, top with the peanut butter cups, gently pressing them down, then cover with the remaining batter. Bake and cool according to package directions.

Using the 3- inch excess foil, transfer the brownie to a cutting board. Cut in half and set one half aside for another use. Cut the remaining half into 1-inch squares.

Using an electric mixer, beat the cream in a medium bowl on high for about 3 minutes or until medium-stiff peaks form.

To assemble the trifles, layer brownies, bananas, whipped cream and caramel in six 8 ounce glasses. Top with whipped cream and peanuts and drizzle with caramel.

· · · · ·

I love trifles and this combination of ingredients can't be beat! This was adapted from a popular recipe found among my collection of peanut butter and banana favorites!

PEANUT BUTTER
AND JELLY DESSERT

· · · · ·

1 box white cake mix
3 egg whites
2 Tablespoons vegetable oil
1 box (4 servings) vanilla
    mousse mix
Brown food coloring

1 Cup strawberry jelly
¼ Cup all-purpose flour
1 and ⅓ Cups water
¾ Cup cold milk
3 Tablespoons creamy-style
    peanut butter

Coat a 15 × 10½ × 1-inch jelly-roll pan with cooking spray.
Line bottom with waxed paper; coat paper with spray. Combine
cake mix and flour in bowl. Prepare following package directions,
using egg whites, water and oil. Scrape into prepared pan.
Bake in 350 degree oven 28-32 minutes, until golden and cake
springs back when touched. Cool in pan on rack. Invert.

Beat mousse and milk in bowl. Add peanut butter; beat until
smooth and slightly thickened, about 4 minutes. Tint lightly
with food coloring. Chill. Melt jelly in small saucepan over low
heat or in microwave oven.

Cut cake lengthwise in half, and then crosswise in half, making a
total of 4 pieces. Slice each piece in half horizontally. Spread jelly
on non-cut sides of 4 bottom pieces. Spread mousse over other 4
pieces. Invert jelly layers onto mousse layers, with rough cut side
facing up. Refrigerate 20 minutes. Cut each sandwich diagonally
into quarters.

· · · · ·

*This is one of your kid's favorite sandwiches elevated to a dessert
sensation! This recipe was adapted from an old magazine.*

TOPPINGS DU JOUR
COOKIE PIZZA

· · · · ·

COOKIE PIZZA
1 (20 oz.) pkg. refrigerated
   sugar cookie dough
1 Cup candy corn

1/2 Cup creamy peanut
   butter
½ Cup raisins

GLAZE
2 to 4 Tablespoons vanilla frosting, melted

Heat oven to 350 degrees. Line 12-inch pizza pan with foil;
grease foil. Cut cookie dough into ¼-inch slices; press slices
into bottom of foil lined pan to form crust. Bake for 15 to 20
minutes or until deep golden brown. Cool completely. Carefully
remove foil from cookie pizza. Spread cookie with peanut butter.
Sprinkle evenly with candy corn and raisins. Drizzle glaze over
pizza. Cut into wedges or squares.

16 to 24 servings.

Tip: To melt frosting in a microwave oven, place in a small
bowl. Microwave on HIGH 10 to 15 seconds or until thin; stir.

· · · · ·

Variations: Using peanut butter chips and chocolate
chips, instead of candy corn and raisins, creates a winning
combination. Choose your own favorite toppings to create a
personalized "toppings du jour cookie pizza."

Source unknown.

PIES

CHOCOLATE PEANUT BUTTER
ICE CREAM PIE

· · · · ·

CRUST

15 chocolate sandwich cookies

¼ Cup butter or margarine,
  melted

½ Cup dry roasted peanuts

FILLING

3 quarts chocolate ice cream,
  softened

1 Cup heavy whipping cream

2 Tablespoons confectioners'
  sugar

7 packages (1.8 ounce each
  or 20 packages (.6 ounce
  each) Reese's Peanut
  Butter Cups, coarsely
  chopped

SAUCE

1 jar (8 ounce) chocolate
  fudge topping

2 Tablespoons coffee-flavor liqueur

¼ Cup strong brewed
  coffee

Preheat oven to 375 degrees. Process cookies with peanuts in
food processor to fine crumbs. Reserve 1 Tablespoon crumbs
for garnish; combine remaining crumbs with melted butter in a
medium bowl. Press in bottom and up sides of 9-inch pie plate.
Bake 10 minutes or until set. If necessary, press into place with a
wooden spoon. Cool on wire rack.

Combine ice cream with chopped peanut butter cups in large
bowl. Spoon into cooled crust. Cover and freeze 6 hours or
overnight.

Beat cream with sugar in small mixer bowl to stiff peaks. Spoon or pipe over top of pie. Sprinkle reserved crumbs on top.

Heat fudge topping in small saucepan until hot; stir in coffee and liqueur.

12 Servings.

. . . . .

Source unknown.

CHOCOLATE
PEANUT BUTTER PIE

· · · · ·

1 Keebler Ready Crust Graham
   Cracker Pie Crust
¼ Cup creamy peanut butter
1 (8 ounce) Cool Whip, thawed

1 (14 ounce) can Eagle Brand
   Creamy Chocolate
   Sweetened Condensed
   Milk

In large bowl, combine sweetened condensed milk and peanut
butter, mix well. Fold in whipped topping. Spoon into crust.
Freeze 6 hours. Garnish as desired.

· · · · ·

Source unknown.

CHOCOLATE PEANUT BUTTER ICE CREAM PIE (LOW FAT)

· · · · ·

¾ Cup nutlike cereal nuggets
  (such as Grape Nuts), divided
1 (2.1 ounce) package chocolate
  sugar-free instant pudding mix
¼ Cup peanut butter

2 Cups chocolate low-fat
  ice cream, slightly
  softened
1 Cup frozen fat-free
  whipped topping,
  thawed

Sprinkle ½ Cup cereal nuggets evenly in bottom of an 8-inch
round cake pan. Combine remaining ¼ Cup cereal nuggets,
ice cream, pudding mix and peanut butter in a large bowl; stir
until mixture is well blended. Fold in whipped topping. Spoon
ice cream mixture into prepared pan, spreading gently with a
spatula. Cover and freeze 2 hours or until firm. Let stand at
room temperature 15 minutes before serving.

· · · · ·

This "free" recipe came in a flyer in the newspaper.

PEANUT BUTTER
CHOCOLATE PIE

· · · · ·

3 eggs
1 Cup light corn syrup
½ Cup sugar
⅓ Cup chunky peanut butter
½ teaspoon vanilla
Chopped peanuts (optional)

½ Cup semi-sweet
    chocolate pieces
Pastry for single-pie crust
Whipped dessert topping
    (optional)
Semi-sweet chocolate pieces
    (optional)

For filling, in a mixing bowl, beat eggs lightly with a fork until combined. Stir in corn syrup, sugar, peanut butter, and vanilla. Mix well. Sprinkle ½ Cup chocolate pieces over the bottom of an unbaked pastry-lined 9-inch pie plate. Pour filling into pie shell. Cover edge of pie with foil. Bake in 375 degree oven for 20 minutes. Remove foil. Bake for 15 to 20 minutes more or until knife inserted near the center comes out clean. Cover and chill to store for up to 48 hours. Garnish with whipped topping, remaining chocolate pieces, and peanuts, if desired.

10 servings.

· · · · ·

This recipe was clipped from a magazine many years ago. My only change to this recipe would be to add peanut butter chips on the pastry-lined pie plate and add some peanut butter chips to the garnish! You can never have too much peanut butter for me!

COUNTRY
PEANUT BUTTER PIE
· · · · ·

CRUST

1½ Cups oatmeal

3 Tablespoons flour

⅓ Cup brown sugar

⅓ Cup melted butter

Spray 9-inch pan with nonstick spray. Mix ingredients and press in pan. Bake at 350 degrees for 20 minutes. Cool completely.

CHOCOLATE FILLING

½ Cup butter, softened

1 egg

¾ teaspoon vanilla

½ Cup chopped peanuts

½ Cup sugar

¾ Cup semi-sweet chocolate chips, melted

Beat butter and sugar; add egg. Beat on medium speed for 3 minutes. Blend in melted chocolate chips and vanilla. Spread cooled crust with 1 cup chocolate filling; sprinkle with ½ cup chopped peanuts.

PEANUT BUTTER FILLING

8 ounce cream cheese

1 Cup powdered sugar

1½ Cups frozen whipped topping, thawed

½ Cup peanut butter

1 egg

¼ Cup chopped peanuts

Beat cream cheese, peanut butter and powdered sugar until smooth and creamy; add egg. Fold in whipped topping. Spoon peanut butter filling over nuts; top with remaining chocolate filling. Sprinkle with ¼ Cup peanuts around outer edge. Refrigerate 3 hours.

· · · · ·

This recipe was taken from a local newspaper and says, "Author unknown, Harrisburg".

CREAM CHEESE
PEANUT BUTTER PIE

. . . . .

CRUST

1 Cup vanilla wafer cookie crumbs   ½ Cup finely chopped pecans
6 Tablespoons butter, melted   2 Tablespoons sugar
⅛ teaspoon cinnamon

Mix all in a 9-inch round pie pan. Press mixture firmly onto
bottom and up sides. Freeze while preparing filling.

FILLING

1¼ Cups peanut butter   1 (8 ounce) cream cheese,
1 Cup powdered sugar   room temperature
2 Tablespoons butter, melted   1¼ Cups whipping cream,
1 Tablespoon vanilla   chilled

Using electric mixer, beat peanut butter, cream cheese and
½ cup of the powdered sugar and melted butter in a large
bowl. Using clean beaters, in separate bowl, beat the 1¼ cups
whipping cream with the other ½ cup powdered sugar and the
Tablespoon of vanilla until peaks form. Stir ¼ of this whipped
cream mixture into the peanut butter mixture. Then fold in
remaining whipped cream/sugar mixture. Spoon into prepared
crust. Refrigerate until firm.

GLAZE

½ Cup whipping cream   4 ounces semi-sweet chocolate

Bring cream to a boil in heavy saucepan. Reduce heat to low. Add chocolate and stir until melted and smooth. Cool glaze slightly. Pour over filling. Tilt pan to cover top completely. Refrigerate at lease one hour.

· · · · ·

My cousin, Joanie Bryner, gave me this recipe. She said "It is a pain to make it, but it's worth it." I agree!

FROZEN
PEANUT BUTTER PIE

· · · · ·

2 Cups Cool Whip, thawed
¼ Cup peanut butter
1 teaspoon vanilla
1 Cup ricotta cheese

½ Cup skim milk
4 to 5 packages Equal
sweetener

Blend all ingredients except Cool Whip. Fold in Cool Whip and pour into crust of your choosing, such as chocolate crumb or graham cracker. Freeze.

· · · · ·

A great variation from the typical Frozen Peanut Butter Pie for those interested in watching calories! Source unknown.

ICE CREAM PIE

· · · · ·

½ Cup light corn syrup
Not quite 2½ Cups
   Rice Krispies

½ Cup peanut butter
A little more than a quart of
   ice cream, Vanilla or Peanut
   Butter Ice Cream or the ice
   cream of your choice

Mix the first three ingredients together. Press into a 9-inch pie pan. Let ice cream get a little soft, then spoon into pie crust. Put back in freezer. Before serving, spoon hot fudge (or for my peanut butter lovin' friends, peanut butter topping) over each piece.

· · · · ·

*This recipe came from Nancy Walborn, from my church, many years ago. Still a **FAVORITE**!*

NATURAL
PEANUT BUTTER PIE

· · · · ·

1 (16 ounce) jar natural
    peanut butter
1 (8 ounce) package ⅓ reduced
    fat cream cheese, softened
¾ Cup honey
1 (8 ounce) container frozen whipped topping, thawed

1 chocolate pie crust
2 Tablespoons semi-
    sweet chocolate chips
½ teaspoon shortening

Beat together cream cheese and honey until well mixed. Stir in
peanut butter; mix well. Gently fold in whipped topping. Spoon
into crust. Heat chocolate chips and shortening over low heat
until melted; drizzle over pie. Chill 4 hours or overnight.

Tip: For even more peanut taste, try chunky pb!

· · · · ·

*A recipe given to me by my friend, Susanne Ryan. Actual source
unknown.*

COOKIE CRUST
FROZEN PEANUT BUTTER PIE

. . . . .

24 Nutter Butter Sandwich
　Cookies
1 (8 ounce) Philadelphia Cream
Cheese, softened
1 Tablespoon vanilla

5 Tablespoons butter, melted
1 Cup peanut butter
¾ Cup sugar
1 (8 ounce) Cool Whip,
　thawed, divided

CRUSH cookies in zipper-style plastic bag with rolling pin or
in food processor. Mix cookie crumbs and butter. Press onto
bottom and sides of 9- inch pie plate. MIX cream cheese,
peanut butter, sugar and vanilla with electric mixer on medium
speed until well blended. Gently stir in 1 and ½ Cups whipped
topping. FREEZE 4 hours or overnight until firm. Let stand
½ hour or until pie can be cut easily. Garnish with remaining
whipped topping and additional cookies, if desired.

Makes 8 servings.

. . . . .

Source unknown.

PEANUT BUTTER AND FUDGE ICE CREAM PIE

. . . . .

½ Cup peanut butter
1 quart vanilla ice cream, softened
½ Cup cashews, chopped
   and divided

¼ Cup honey
Graham cracker pie crust
½ Cup fudge topping,
   warmed

Garnish: whipped topping, additional warmed fudge topping and chopped cashews.

Combine peanut butter and honey; stir in ice cream. Spoon half of ice- cream mixture into pie crust; sprinkle with half of cashews. Drizzle ¼ Cup fudge topping over cashews. Spoon remaining ice cream mixture over top. Sprinkle with remaining cashews and drizzle with remaining fudge topping. Freeze about 8 hours or until firm. Top with garnish, if desired.

Serves 6 to 8.

. . . . .

This was a free recipe that came in the mail and is almost identical to a Keebler 15-Minute P.B. and Fudge Ice Cream Pie recipe that I have.

PEANUT BUTTER CREAM PIE

. . . . .

1 (8 ounce) package cream cheese,
  softened
6 Tablespoons milk
1 Graham cracker crust
¼ Cup chopped peanuts

¾ Cup confectioners'
  sugar
½ Cup peanut butter
1 (8 ounce) frozen whipped
  topping, thawed

In a mixing bowl, beat cream cheese until fluffy. Add sugar
and peanut butter; mix well. Gradually add the milk. Fold in
whipped topping; spoon into the crust. Sprinkle with peanuts.
Chill overnight.

6 to 8 Servings.

. . . . .

Source unknown.

PEANUT BUTTER PIE #1

. . . . .

¾ Cup chocolate fudge
   topping, divided
1 (8 ounce) Cool Whip, thawed
1¼ Cups cold milk
½ Cup peanut butter
1 Keebler Ready Crust

Graham Cracker Pie
   Crust
2 packages (4-Serving
   Size) Jell-O Vanilla
   Flavor Instant Pudding
   and Pie Filling

SPOON ½ Cup fudge sauce into bottom of pie crust. Gently spread ½ of the whipped topping over fudge sauce; place in freezer 10 minutes. POUR milk into large bowl; stir in peanut butter until smooth. Add pudding mixes. Beat with wire whisk 2 minutes or until smooth (Mixture will be thick). Immediately stir in remaining whipped topping. Scoop over layers in pie crust.

REFRIGERATE 3 hours or until set. To serve, drizzle with remaining fudge topping.

Makes 8 servings.

. . . . .

This recipe came from my friend, Susanne Ryan, and there is no documentation to its origin.

PEANUT BUTTER PIE #2

. . . . .

1 Cup peanut butter
1 Cup powdered sugar

1 (8 ounce) cream cheese
2 (8 ounce) Cool Whip, thawed

Mix all ingredients, folding in the Cool Whip last. Spoon into a graham cracker or chocolate crust. Freeze. Thaw 10 to 15 minutes before serving.

. . . . .

I found this recipe on a small piece of paper (3" × 3") and remember making it many times! I have no idea who gave it to me though!

PEANUT BUTTER PIE #3

· · · · ·

4 heaping Tablespoons peanut butter
½ teaspoon vanilla
1 large frozen whipped topping,
    thawed

1 (8 ounce) cream cheese
½ pound powdered
    sugar

Mix all together and put in 9-inch baked pie shell. Top with chopped peanuts. Chill completely.

· · · · ·

A slight variation of ingredients from other Peanut Butter Pie recipes, but just as delicious as the others! I have no documentation as to where the recipe originated.

PEANUT BUTTER CUP
MINI-PIES

. . . . .

6 mini graham cracker shells
24 Reese's Peanut Butter Cups
    Miniatures, unwrapped
    peanut butter chips

Sliced bananas
1½ Cups miniature
    marshmallows

Place shells in large metal baking pan. Place 3 banana slices and 3 Miniatures in each shell. Top each with ¼ Cup marshmallows and some peanut butter chips. Bake at 375 degrees for 8 minutes or until hot and bubbly.

Remove and top each with 1 Miniature. Cool slightly; serve warm.

Serves 6.

. . . . .

This recipe was modified from a recipe found on a Reese's Peanut Butter Cup Miniatures package.

QUEEN ANN'S CHOCOLATE
PEANUT BUTTER PIE

· · · · ·

22 Oreo Chocolate Sandwich
  Cookies, finely crushed
1 Cup sliced bananas (about
  2 medium)
1 1/2 Cups whipped topping
1/2 Cup creamy peanut butter

3 Cups milk
1/4 Cup butter or margarine,
  melted
2 (4 serving size) packages
  Royal Instant Chocolate
  Pudding and Pie Filling

Mix cookie crumbs with margarine or butter. Press firmly on bottom and side of 9-inch pie plate; refrigerate 30 minutes. Spread peanut butter over bottom of prepared crust. Arrange bananas over peanut butter; set aside. Beat pudding mix and milk in medium bowl with a mixer at low speed for 1 minute. Pour pudding over bananas. Refrigerate at least 2 hours before serving. Top pie with whipped topping. Garnish as desired.

· · · · ·

This recipe was taken from the coupon insert in the Sunday Paper. Source unknown.

SUNDAES AND TOPPINGS

PEANUT BUTTER CHOCOLATE
S'MORE SUNDAES

· · · · ·

¼ Cup semi-sweet chocolate chips
¼ Cup half-and-half
1 pint vanilla ice cream
4 (2½ inches) squares graham
   crackers, coarsely crushed

¼ Cup peanut butter chips
1½ Tablespoons butter or
   margarine
¼ Cup miniature
   marshmallows

In small saucepan over low heat combine semi-sweet chocolate chips, peanut butter chips, half-and-half and butter or margarine, stirring constantly until melted and smooth. Remove from heat and cool slightly. Divide vanilla ice cream among 4 individual serving dishes. Place in freezer until ready to serve. Just before serving pour 2 Tablespoons of warm peanut butter/chocolate sauce over each serving of ice cream. Sprinkle with coarsely crushed graham cracker squares and miniature marshmallows.

Makes 4 servings.

· · · · ·

This recipe was taken from a paper insert found at the grocery store and modified by me. I added the peanut butter to create a more satisfying dessert for the peanut butter lover!

PEANUT-FUDGE
SAUCE

· · · · ·

1 Cup chocolate syrup
Vanilla or Chocolate Ice Cream

¼ Cup chunky peanut
butter

Stir chocolate syrup into peanut butter. Serve sauce over ice cream.

· · · · ·

This recipe came from a fundraising cookbook given to me by my sister many years ago.

HOT PLANTATION
SUNDAE SAUCE

. . . . .

¼ pound butter
1 5⅓ ounce can evaporated
   milk

Vanilla ice cream
2 Cups (packed) brown sugar
1 Cup peanut butter

Melt butter in saucepan over low heat; add brown sugar gradually. Add milk and peanut butter; cook until well blended. Serve warm over ice cream. Remaining sauce keeps well in covered container in refrigerator.

Makes 2½ Cups.

. . . . .

This recipe came from the same fundraising cookbook given to me by my sister.

I DARE YOU!

PEANUT BUTTER
AND KETCHUP SANDWICH

. . . . .

2 slices of your   Peanut butter
   favorite bread   Ketchup

Spread peanut butter and ketchup on bread and try it! **I dare you!**

. . . . .

My Uncle Jack Frost knew I was saving recipes for a cookbook and told me about the above recipe. In the nearly 20 years I have been collecting recipes, I waited to try this one until the end. My husband kept saying Uncle Jack was "pulling my leg," but Uncle Jack insisted he wasn't. He always had a smile on his face and said "Try it." So I finally tried it in February of 2014, and while I wouldn't put it on "my fav" list, I can say I tried it and it wasn't bad. So I dare you!

SOME FACTS ABOUT PEANUT BUTTER
· · · · ·

Americans eat more peanut butter than anyone else; more than 75 percent of families in the United States typically buy peanut butter throughout the year.

Peanut butter offers many sources of vitamins and minerals: vitamins E and B6, niacin, thiamin, riboflavin, copper, phosphorus, potassium, zinc and magnesium. It is also a good source of protein and fiber.

The creamy spread was first introduced in 1890 when a St. Louis physician came up with the idea to turn peanuts into a nutritious meal substitute.

Women and children prefer creamy peanut butter, while most men opt for chunky.

East Coasters buy more creamy peanut butter, while West Coasters prefer it chunky.

It takes 540 peanuts to make a 12 ounce jar of peanut butter.

By law, any product labeled "peanut butter" in the United States must be at least 90% peanuts.

The world's largest peanut butter factory churns out 250,000 jars every day.

Four of the top 10 candy bars manufactured in the United States contain peanuts or peanut butter.

Americans spend $800 million a year on peanut butter.

The average peanut farm is 100 acres.

The average American consumes more than 6 pounds of peanuts and peanut butter products a year.

The average child will eat an average of 1500 peanut butter and jelly sandwiches before he/she graduates from high school.

Two peanut farmers have been elected President of the USA— Thomas Jefferson and Jimmy Carter.

As the "Father of the Peanut Industry," George Washington Carver developed more than 300 uses for peanuts.

There are 4 types of peanuts grown in the United States— Runner, which is an attractive uniform kernel, Virginia, which is the largest of all peanut varieties, Spanish, which is small with red-brown skin and Valencia, which has 3 or more small kernels and bright red skin.

· · · · ·

I used various sources to obtain this information, collected over many years. Predominantly, though, the information came from the National Peanut Board.org.

HOMEMADE PEANUT BUTTER
· · · · ·

Place 2 Cups salted or unsalted roasted peanuts in blender container. Cover and blend on low speed until finely chopped, about 1 minute. Blend on high speed, stopping blender occasionally to scrape sides, until smooth, about 7 minutes. Cover and refrigerate. Makes about 1 Cup. 115 Calories per tablespoon.

FOOD PROCESSOR DIRECTIONS: Place nuts in work-bowl fitted with steel blade. Cover and process until smooth, stopping if necessary to scrape sides, about 3 minutes.

· · · · ·

You will find similar recipes in many cookbooks and on the internet. The actual source for this recipe is unknown.

CONCLUSION

· · · · ·

This is the end, or is it? Actually, it could be just the beginning. It is definitely the end of **Volume I of "Peanut Butter Passion,"** but it is not the end of my peanut butter recipes. With the collection of recipes I still have, those that I may continue to accumulate, the ones my friends continue to send me and those that I might receive from you, the reader, **there could be a Volume II.** No promises, because as much fun as this journey has been, it took time, energy, commitment and dedication. After 20 plus years of saving recipes, it took me over two years to complete the project. I can honestly say, I am "buggy eyed" from checking and rechecking these 100 plus recipes. For now, it's time for me to share my joy with you and for you to begin testing and tasting the many delicious recipes compiled in this **labor of love!**

If you have a favorite recipe you would like to share, please send it to me via e-mail at **PeanutButterPassion7@gmail.com.** My receipt of the recipe is your permission for me to use it, if I do begin **Volume II.** If I don't, trust me when I tell you that I will try each and every recipe I receive. I love the taste of peanut butter and will continue to find joy in trying new recipes with **peanut butter** as the key ingredient.

GIFT GIVING—If you know someone with a passion for peanut butter, baking or cooking, this is a **"CAN'T GO WRONG GIFT!"** It will delight the **"Peanut Butter Lover!"**

For those who have purchased this cookbook or received it as a gift, I hope you get the same joy and pleasure, in making, tasting, sharing and enjoying these recipes, as I did.

FUNDRAISING—If you are interested in selling this cookbook as a fundraising project, please contact me at the e-mail address listed above.

INDEX

· · · · ·